Free Talking
Basic Strategies for Building Communication

Adam Gyenes
Matthew Guay
Lauren Eldekvist
Yuki Hasegawa

Australia • Brazil • Mexico • Singapore • United Kingdom • United States

Free Talking—Basic Strategies for Building Communication

Adam Gyenes / Matthew Guay / Lauren Eldekvist / Yuki Hasegawa

© 2019 Cengage Learning K.K.

ALL RIGHTS RESERVED. No part of this work covered by the copyright herein may be reproduced, transmitted, stored, or used in any form or by any means—graphic, electronic, or mechanical, including but not limited to photocopying, recording, scanning, digitizing, taping, Web distribution, information networks, or information storage and retrieval systems—without the prior written permission of the publisher.

"National Geographic", "National Geographic Society" and the Yellow Border Design are registered trademarks of the National Geographic Society ® Marcas Registradas

Photo credits appear on page 144, which constitutes a continuation of the copyright page.

For permission to use material from this textbook or product, e-mail to **eltjapan@cengage.com**

ISBN: 978-4-86312-349-6

National Geographic Learning | Cengage Learning K.K.
No. 2 Funato Building 5th Floor
1-11-11 Kudankita, Chiyoda-ku
Tokyo 102-0073
Japan

Tel: 03-3511-4392
Fax: 03-3511-4391

Acknowledgments:
The authors and publisher would like to thank Lucius Von Joo, Robert J. Werner, Midori Teramoto, Ryoko Ohata, and Yukihiro Fujita for their contributions to this textbook.

Preface

Welcome to *Free Talking*! The way young people in the US and other English-speaking countries talk to each other may be somewhat different from the English that you have learned at school. We have designed this textbook so that you can enjoy talking with your classmates while practicing the kinds of daily conversations you would actually have if you were a student at a university in the US. A lot of textbooks ask you to role play situations and use language that is unnatural for students. However, *Free Talking* uses topics and situations common to students all over the world, so you can learn to express the real you. We feel that you can have fun speaking English by learning the key words and phrases that let you tell others how you really feel and what you do in your daily life. This textbook includes basic expressions that are useful in a variety of situations allowing you to hold conversations with overseas students even if your vocabulary is limited.

The main characters are six students from around the world attending North Beach University, Hawaii. Each unit includes a comic model of the students holding a conversation that typically happen around college towns. We hope you can see yourself in some of these characters and enjoy following the models with your classmates. We believe that by practicing many simple conversations, you can increase speaking confidence, learn to add more details, and ask your classmates more questions whatever your English level.

When talking with people from overseas, Japanese people often feel they lack the simple words and expressions that would make the conversation more fun and relaxing. We believe *Free Talking* will not only make your lessons enjoyable, but also give you the English you need to enjoy talking with people your own age all over the world.

皆さんの中には、アメリカなどの英語圏の国の若者の会話と、学校で習ってきた英語がなんとなく違っていると感じる方がいるかもしれません。本書の執筆のきっかけは、アメリカの大学生が日常的に交わしているような英会話を、皆さん自身がクラスメートと楽しめるようになればいいなと思ったことです。学生には違和感がある会話演習を求める英語教材が多々ありますが、本書では世界中の学生に共通の話題や状況を扱っていますので、皆さんにとって等身大の英語表現を学ぶことができるでしょう。楽しく英語で話せるようになるには、日常生活での出来事や思いを伝えるために必要不可欠な語句を習得することです。本書ではさまざまな場面で役立つ基本表現を紹介していますので、豊富な語彙力がなくても、海外の学生たちと会話ができるようになるでしょう。

本書の主な登場人物は世界各国からハワイにやってきた6人の学生で、ノースビーチ大学に通っています。ユニットごとに掲載しているマンガでは、キャンパスやその周辺で学生がよく交わす会話をモデルとして紹介しています。登場人物との共通点を見つけながら、クラスメートとの会話練習を楽しんでください。英語の習熟度に関係なく、誰でも簡単な会話を繰り返し練習することで話す自信がつきますし、詳しく説明する方法を学んだり、たくさん質問することができたりするようにもなるでしょう。

日本人の多くが外国人と話をするときに感じることは、会話を楽しむために必要な簡単な語彙力が身についていないということです。本書を使うことで授業が楽しくなることはもちろん、皆さんが世界中の同世代の若者と気軽に言葉を交わせる英語力を習得できるようになることを願っています。

Adam Gyenes (ed.)
Matthew Guay
Lauren Eldekvist
長谷川由貴

Table of Contents

Page		
3	Preface	
6	To the Teacher	
9	Seven Characters	

Page	Unit	Title	Functions	Short Talk
10	Unit 1	**Introductions**	• Getting to know someone • Talking about personal information	Self-introductions in class
16	Unit 2	**Daily Life**	• Talking about routines • Describing frequency	Breakfast
22	Unit 3	**Weekend Events**	• Showing interest and feelings • Asking follow-up questions	Favorite weekend activities
30	Unit 4	**Small Talk**	• Greeting people • Continuing a conversation	Part-time jobs
36	Unit 5	**Likes and Dislikes**	• Talking about preferences • Giving reasons	Activities on Sunday morning
42	Unit 6	**Student Life**	• Talking about needs and wants • Recommending places	Today's events
52	Unit 7	**Family**	• Describing appearance • Talking about similarity	Future image
60	Unit 8	**Friends**	• Talking about personality • Giving examples	Individual personality
66	Unit 9	**Going Out**	• Talking about free time • Arranging schedules	A favorite place to go with friends

Page	Unit	Title	Functions	Short Talk
74	Unit 10	**Restaurants**	▪ Ordering food and drinks ▪ Talking about problems	The last restaurant I went to
80	Unit 11	**Shopping**	▪ Talking about shopping places ▪ Responding to suggestions	Opinions about shopping
86	Unit 12	**Strengths and Weaknesses**	▪ Asking for help ▪ Talking about abilities	Personal skills
94	Unit 13	**Places**	▪ Describing features ▪ Talking about upsides and downsides	Hometown
100	Unit 14	**Vacations**	▪ Talking about travel plans ▪ Explaining intentions	Vacation plans
106	Unit 15	**Experiences**	▪ Talking about past events ▪ Describing feelings	Memories from a trip
116	Unit 16	**Opinions**	▪ Making comparisons ▪ Agreeing and disagreeing	The best way to relax
122	Unit 17	**Health and Illness**	▪ Talking about health problems ▪ Giving advice	Good health habits
130	Unit 18	**The Future**	▪ Talking about dreams and goals ▪ Making time references	Future plans

28	Review of Units 1–3
50	Review of Units 4–6
72	Review of Units 7–9
92	Review of Units 10–12
114	Review of Units 13–15
136	Review of Units 16–18
138	Vocabulary List
143	Useful Expressions

To the Teacher

This textbook is designed to be a universal speaking course to maximize opportunities for students to speak together with many pair-work activities. The lessons are designed with flexibility and adaptability in mind so that they will suit large or small class settings and cater to students with various backgrounds, interests, and motivation levels.

There are six sections in each unit. Some may be focused on or omitted to optimize the lesson for different levels and classes. Each unit has been designed with a conversation model and scaffolded activities in early stages, to allow basic level students to develop the solid foundation they need to enjoy speaking, but also provide opportunities to expand conversations and develop fluency. Activities towards the end of each unit encourage freer speaking, personalization, and fluency building.

Unit Overview

This textbook is divided into 18 units. A review unit follows every three units. Based on the one class a week, 90-minute lesson, 15-week semester common at many universities in Japan, it is assumed teachers will be able to cover the first half of the textbook in one semester.

Preparation

This section includes exercises intended to be completed before the start of class, providing students with knowledge of words and expressions they will use throughout the lesson. There is also a warm-up speaking activity that all students can participate in easily, having completed previous tasks.

Conversation Model

This section shows students how the target language is used in a comic conversation. This includes gap-fills, so students read the comic and fill in the blanks. They can also listen to the conversation, read it with a partner, and read again with substitutions. Teachers may also wish to use the comic and audio for pronunciation and pattern practice.

Practice

At the start of this section, target expressions are listed so that students can easily refer to them throughout the following activities. Practice activities are scaffolded pair-work activities to allow students to gradually progress from highly controlled language use, closely resembling the conversation model, to freer use of the target language.

Expanded Conversation

Having practiced the target expressions in the previous sections, these activities allow students to use their new language knowledge to complete a task-based activity and an opportunity to mingle with other classmates.

Short Talk

The aim of this section is to develop more fluent use of English without dependence on a conversation model, and for students to gain some basic presentation skills in a low-pressure setting. It is intended to challenge students and for a class of basic level students, teachers may wish to omit this section or alter the way activities are used.

Listening

Students listen to monologues that provide a model for the short talk in the following speaking task. While the audio recordings present natural, fluent language use, listening tasks are relatively simple.

Speaking

The short talk topic is the same as the listening tasks that students have completed. Students prepare notes which they use to perform a personalized talk, using language they have studied throughout the unit. Short talks can be performed in small groups, ideally with four to six students in each group. The difficulty of this activity can be adjusted for different classes: Stronger students can be challenged to perform their talk without looking at notes. For basic level classes, question prompts can be used for small group discussions instead of short talks.

Wrap-up

This is a quick wrap-up activity that helps the students reflect on the lesson and think about what they want to remember. It could be expanded into a speaking activity, but is mostly intended for self-reflection.

Downloadable Audio Files

Please explain the following instructions to your students.

For activities with a headset icon (🎧), audio files are available at

https://ngljapan.com/freetalking-audio/

You can download audio files (MP3) to your computer as outlined below.
1. Visit the website above.
2. Click the link to the file you would like to download.

Use the QR code to directly access audio files.

Seven Characters

In every unit, you will listen to a conversation and short talks featuring the characters from North Beach University, Hawaii.

Shin Kawamoto
Shin is from Chiba in Japan. He is an exchange student and will stay for one year to study English. His major in Japan is international tourism and he wants to be a tour guide in the future. He plays the bass guitar and likes baseball.

Mark Franklin
Mark is from New York in the US. He is roommates with Shin. He studies information systems and is a sophomore. He likes basketball, comics, and video games.

Dan Blake
Dan is from Christchurch in New Zealand. He studies Japanese and is a junior. He works part-time in a Japanese restaurant. He has never been to Japan but really wants to go someday. He practices kendo.

Alice Canty
Alice is from Brighton in the UK. She studies psychology and is a freshman. She is very active and enjoys running, yoga, and jiu-jitsu. She also loves traveling and wants to go to South America someday.

June Yang
June is from Shanghai in China. She studies art and design, and is a senior. She likes photography and wants to be a comic artist in the future. She loves cats.

Mariko Nakamura
Mariko is from Yokohama in Japan. She is an exchange student and will study in Hawaii for one year to get a Japanese teaching license. She wants to be a Japanese teacher in the future. She loves surfing and snowboarding.

Yolanda Turner
Yolanda is a professor and teaches social studies. The six students are all taking her class. She is from California and just moved to Hawaii for her new job at North Beach University.

Unit 1
Introductions
Getting to know someone | Talking about personal information

Preparation

A Write the subject matching each picture.

- art and design
- healthcare
- international tourism
- psychology
- sports science
- economics
- information systems
- law
- social studies

1. _____

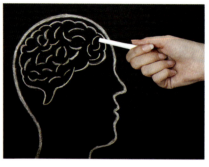
2. _____

3. _____

4. _____

5. _____

6. _____

7. _____

8. _____

9. _____

Introductions Unit 1

B Look at the Seven Characters section on page 9. Then answer the questions below.

1. How many of the students are from Japan? _____
2. Which student is from the US? _____
3. Which student is studying art and design? _____
4. Which student likes surfing? _____
5. Where is North Beach University? _____
6. What is the name of the professor? _____

C Complete the student ID card with your own information.

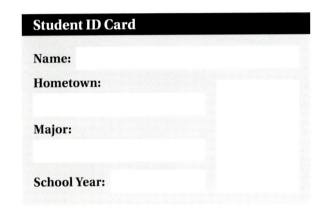

Student ID Card

Name:

Hometown:

Major:

School Year:

D Work in pairs. Student A, ask your partner the questions below. Student B, answer the questions with your own information. Change roles and practice again.

1. What's your name?
   My name is …

2. Where are you from?
   I'm from …

3. What's your major?
   My major is …

4. What year are you in?
   I'm a …

11

Conversation Model

A Fill in the blanks with the words below. Then listen to the conversation and check your answers.

- from
- major
- name
- whereabouts

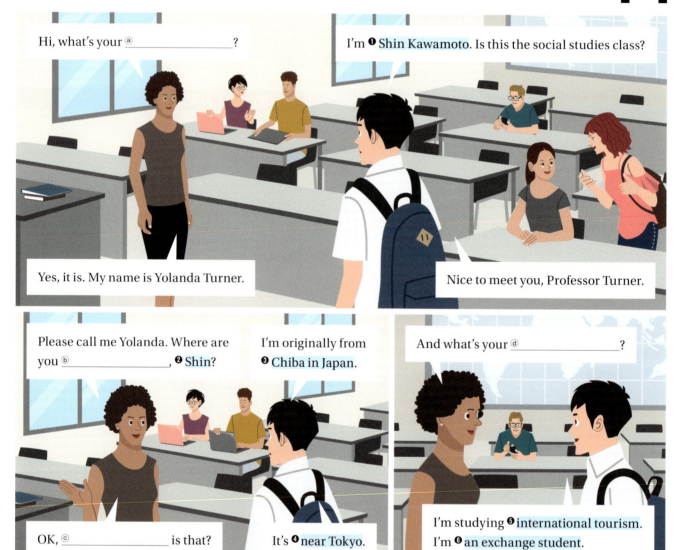

Hi, what's your ⓐ_____?

I'm ❶ Shin Kawamoto. Is this the social studies class?

Yes, it is. My name is Yolanda Turner.

Nice to meet you, Professor Turner.

Please call me Yolanda. Where are you ⓑ_____, ❷ Shin?

I'm originally from ❸ Chiba in Japan.

And what's your ⓓ_____?

OK, ⓒ_____ is that?

It's ❹ near Tokyo.

I'm studying ❺ international tourism. I'm ❻ an exchange student.

B Work in pairs. Read the conversation with your partner. Change roles once. Then practice again with the substitutions below.

[Substitution 1] ❶ Alice Canty ❷ Alice ❸ Brighton in the UK
❹ by the sea ❺ psychology ❻ a freshman

[Substitution 2] ❶ Mark Franklin ❷ Mark ❸ Westchester in New York
❹ north of New York City ❺ information systems ❻ a sophomore

Introductions Unit 1

Practice

🎧 03

Name	
▪ What's your name?	▪ My name is Shin Kawamoto.
Hometown	
▪ Where are you from?	▪ I'm from Shanghai in China.
	▪ I'm originally from Chiba, Japan.
	▪ I was born in the UK.
	▪ I grew up in New Zealand.
Location	
▪ Whereabouts is that?	▪ It's near Tokyo.
	▪ It's in the south/north/east/west of New York City.
	▪ It's in the countryside/suburbs/city.
Major	
▪ What's your major?	▪ My major is economics.
▪ What are you studying?	▪ I major in psychology.
	▪ I'm studying sports science.
School Year	
▪ What year are you in?	▪ I'm a freshman/sophomore/junior/senior.
	▪ I'm a first/second/third/fourth year.
	▪ I'm an exchange student.

A Work in pairs. Student A, ask your partner about his/her name, hometown, its location, major, and school year. Student B, choose one of the cards below and answer the questions. Change roles and practice again.

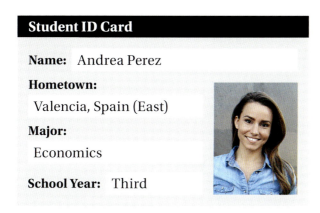

Student ID Card

Name: Andrea Perez
Hometown:
  Valencia, Spain (East)
Major:
  Economics
School Year: Third

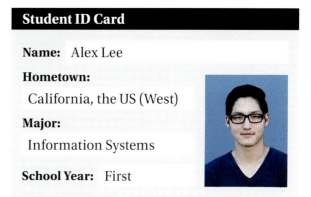

Student ID Card

Name: Alex Lee
Hometown:
  California, the US (West)
Major:
  Information Systems
School Year: First

B Change your partner and practice again using the cards below.

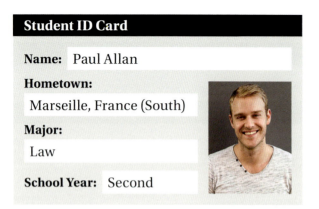

Student ID Card
Name: Paul Allan
Hometown: Marseille, France (South)
Major: Law
School Year: Second

Student ID Card
Name: Keiko Noda
Hometown: Akita, Japan (North)
Major: Sports Science
School Year: Fourth

Expanded Conversation

A Talk to four classmates. Ask them questions to complete the student ID cards.

Student ID Card
Name:
Hometown: (   )
Major:
School Year:

Student ID Card
Name:
Hometown: (   )
Major:
School Year:

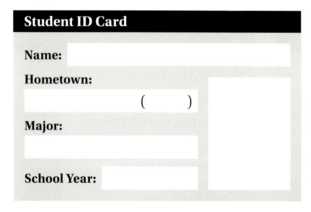

Student ID Card
Name:
Hometown: (   )
Major:
School Year:

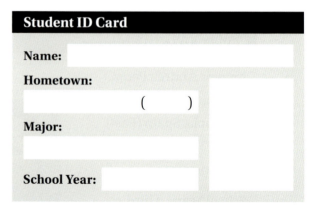

Student ID Card
Name:
Hometown: (   )
Major:
School Year:

B Work in pairs. Look at the conversation on page 12. Student A, take the role of Yolanda. Student B, take the role of Shin. Then make a conversation with your own information. Change roles and practice again.

Introductions Unit 1

Short Talk — Self-introductions in class

Listening

A Listen to the self-introductions by Dan, June, and Mariko. Then match their names to the greetings. 🎧 04–06

It's a pleasure to meet you. •
What's up? •
Nice to meet you. •
Hi, there. •
How's it going? •
It's great to meet you. •
Hello. •
How are you? •

• **Dan** •
• **June** •
• **Mariko** •

• art and design
• cats
• Christchurch, New Zealand
• comic artist
• Japanese teacher
• Shanghai, China
• surfing
• third year student

B Listen again and match their names to their information. 🎧 04–06

Speaking

A Take some notes below and prepare for your self-introduction.

[Greeting] _____ [School Year] _____
[Name] _____ [Major] _____
[Hometown] _____ [Family] _____
[Likes] _____
[Future Dream] _____

B Work in groups. Take turns to give a self-introduction.

Wrap-up

A Complete the sentence by circling one of the words.
This unit was [fun / useful / difficult].

B Write two words/expressions from this unit that you want to remember.
1. _____ 2. _____

15

Unit 2

Daily Life

Talking about routines ⟩ Describing frequency

Preparation

A Write the words matching each picture.

- ask the teacher a question
- fall asleep in class
- hang out with friends
- skip class
- text in class
- drink coffee
- get a high score on a test
- oversleep
- take a bath

1. _____

2. _____

3. _____

4. _____

5. _____

6. _____

7. _____

8. _____

9. _____

B Complete the sentences with your own ideas.

1. I always _____ in the morning.
2. I usually _____ in the evening.
3. I sometimes _____ at night.
4. I hardly ever _____ on the weekend.
5. I never _____ in class.
6. I _____ once a week.
7. I _____ three times a week.
8. I _____ once every two weeks.

C Work in pairs. Student A, ask your partner the questions below. Student B, answer the questions with your ideas from Task B. Change roles and practice again.

1. What do you do in the morning?
   I always …

2. What do you do in the evening?
   I usually …

3. What do you do on the weekend?
   I sometimes …

4. What do you never do in class?
   I never …

5. What do you do once a week?
   I …

Conservation Model

 A Fill in the blanks with the words below. Then listen to the conversation and check your answers.

- actually
- going
- really
- see

How's it ⓐ _____, Mark? Do you want ❶ some eggs?

No thanks, Shin. I ⓑ _____ ❷ never eat breakfast in the morning.

Well, I ❸ always stay up late studying, but then I ❹ usually oversleep in the morning.

Oh, ⓒ _____? Why?

I ⓓ _____.

B Work in pairs. Read the conversation with your partner. Change roles once. Then practice again with the substitutions below.

[Substitution 1]	❶ to go to a party tonight	❷ hardly ever enjoy parties
	❸ often meet new people	❹ can never get a girlfriend
[Substitution 2]	❶ me to fill up the bath	❷ never take a bath at night
	❸ usually just brush my teeth before bed	
	❹ often take a shower in the morning	

Practice

Asking about Routines

- **What do you do** in the morning?
- **What do you never do** at night?
- **How often do you** hang out with your friends?
- **Do you usually** get a high score on a test?

Describing Frequency

[General Expressions]

100%	I **always** watch TV at night.
80%	I **usually** stay up late on Friday.
70%	I **often** study in the library.
30%	I **sometimes** forget to do my homework.
10%	I **occasionally** go to a party.
5%	I **hardly ever** oversleep.
0%	I **never** fall asleep in English class.

[Specific Expressions]
- I get up early **once/twice a** week.
- I brush my teeth **three times a** day.
- I eat breakfast **every day**.
- I go to a coffee shop **every** Sunday.
- I enjoy karaoke **every** two months.

A Make your own sentences with some expressions for frequency.

Ex ask the teacher a question ▶ I always ask the teacher a question in English class.

1. forget to do my homework ▶ _____
2. get a high score on a test ▶ _____
3. skip class ▶ _____
4. go to hot springs ▶ _____
5. drink coffee ▶ _____
6. play video games ▶ _____

B Work in pairs. Practice talking about your school life. Use these words and the expressions for frequency.

- ask the teacher a question
- come to class early
- come to class late
- come to class on time
- fall asleep in class
- forget to do your homework
- get a high score on a test
- skip class
- text in class

Ex A: **Do you usually** come to class early?
    B: I **sometimes** come to class early. How about you?
    A: I come to class early **every day**.

C Change your partner. This time, practice talking about other daily life topics.

- brush my teeth
- eat at a family restaurant
- get up early
- go to a party
- oversleep
- study in the library
- cook dinner
- eat breakfast
- go shopping
- go to hot springs
- play video games
- take a bath
- drink coffee
- enjoy karaoke
- go to a coffee shop
- hang out with friends
- stay up late

Ex A: **How often do you** go to a party?
    B: I go to a party **once a month**. How about you?
    A: I **hardly ever** go to a party.

Expanded Conversation

A Complete questions 4–6 with your own ideas.

Questions	Classmate 1	Classmate 2	Classmate 3
1. What do you do on Saturday night?			
2. Do you usually come to class on time?			
3. How often do you take a bath?			
4. What do you do			
5. Do you usually			
6. How often do you			

B Talk to three classmates. Ask them questions 1–6 and make notes of their answers.

Daily Life Unit 2

Short Talk ▸ Breakfast

Listening

A Listen to the short talks by Mariko and Dan. Then circle the correct answers for question 1.

	Mariko	Dan
1. How often do they eat breakfast?	a. Always b. Sometimes c. Usually	a. Always b. Hardly ever c. Never
2. What is their favorite breakfast food?		

B Listen again and answer question 2.

Speaking

A Prepare for a short talk about your breakfast.

- How often do you eat breakfast?   _____
- What do you usually eat?   _____
- What is your favorite breakfast food?   _____
- How often do you eat it?   _____

B Work in groups. Take turns to give a short talk.

Wrap-up

A Complete the sentences with the words for frequency.

1. I _____ study English at home.
2. I _____ study English on the train.

B Write two words/expressions from this unit that you want to remember.

1. _____   2. _____

21

Unit 3 Weekend Events

Showing interest and feelings ⟩ **Asking follow-up questions**

Preparation

A Complete the list of reactions.

- Awesome!
- I see.
- Lucky you!
- No way!
- Oh, no!
- That's terrible!
- Uh-huh.
- You're joking!

[Good News]
1. _____
2. _____
   That's great!
   That's nice.

[Bad News]
   I'm sorry to hear that.
3. _____
4. _____
   That's too bad.

[Surprising News]
5. _____
   Really?
   That's crazy!
6. _____

[Everyday News]
7. _____
   Oh, yeah?
   OK.
8. _____

B Reorder the words and complete the follow-up questions.

1. I went shopping on Saturday.
   - Who { with / you / go / did }? ▸ Who _____?
   - Where { you / did / go }? ▸ Where _____?
   - What { buy / did / you }? ▸ What _____?

2. I watched a movie last night.
   - What { movie / kind / did / you / watch / of }?
     ▸ What _____?
   - What { the / movie / was / the / name / of }?
     ▸ What _____?
   - Did { enjoy / you / it }? ▸ Did _____?

22

Weekend Events Unit 3

C **Read the events below and write follow-up questions.**

1. I won the lottery.

   ▶ _____

2. My phone got broken.

   ▶ _____

3. I got a new pet.

   ▶ _____

4. I went to a new restaurant yesterday.

   ▶ _____

D **Work in pairs. Student A, tell your partner the events below. Student B, respond with reaction and your follow-up questions from Task C. Change roles and practice again.**

1. I won the lottery.

   Lucky you! ...?

2. My phone got broken.

   That's too bad. ...?

3. I got a new pet.

   Really? ...?

4. I went to a new restaurant yesterday.

   Oh, yeah? ...?

Conversation Model

A Fill in the blanks with the words below. Then listen to the conversation and check your answers.

- phone
- nothing
- Sunday
- weekend

How was your ⓐ_____, June?

Pretty good. I stayed at home on Saturday and ❶had lunch with Dan on ⓑ_____.

❷Had lunch with Dan? That's nice. What kind of ❸food did you eat?

Japanese. It was great. Anyway, what's new?

Oh, ⓒ_____ much, but my phone got ❹broken.

Your ⓓ_____? Really? ❺How did you break it?

❻I dropped it in the bathtub.

❼You're joking! I'm sorry to hear that.

B Work in pairs. Read the conversation with your partner. Change roles once. Then practice again with the substitutions below.

[Substitution 1] ❶ watched a movie ❷ Watched a movie ❸ movie did you watch
❹ lost ❺ Where did you lose it? ❻ I left it on the bus. ❼ No way!

[Substitution 2] ❶ went to a festival ❷ Went to a festival ❸ festival did you go to
❹ stolen ❺ Where was it stolen? ❻ At the library. ❼ That's crazy!

24

Weekend Events Unit 3

Practice

Echo

A: **I ate lunch with Dan** on Sunday.
B: **Ate lunch with Dan?**

A: It was my sister's birthday **last weekend**.
B: **Last weekend?**

Reaction

[Good News]
- Awesome!
- Lucky you!
- That's great!
- That's nice.

[Bad News]
- I'm sorry to hear that.
- Oh, no!
- That's terrible!
- That's too bad.

[Surprising News]
- No way!
- Really?
- That's crazy!
- You're joking!

[Everyday News]
- I see.
- Oh, yeah?
- OK.
- Uh-huh.

Follow-up Questions

Where did you watch it?

What kind of movie did you watch?

Who did you go with?

I watched an interesting movie.

What was the name of the movie?

When did you watch it?

How much did it cost?

Did you enjoy it?

  Read each event below and write your response with an echo, reaction, and follow-up question.

Ex A: My phone was **stolen**.
B: **Stolen? That's terrible. Where** did it happen**?**

1. A: I bought a new bicycle.
   B: _____

2. A: I lost my bag.
   B: _____

3. A: I ate a sandwich.
   B: _____

B Work in pairs. Student A, tell your partner the events from Task A. Student B, respond to them. Change roles and practice again.

25

Expanded Conversation

A Look at the pictures and write sentences about weekend events.

Ex  I went to my part-time job on Saturday and played video games with my friends on Sunday.

1.  _____

2.  _____

3.  _____

B Work in pairs. Student A, ask your partner about weekend events. Use echo, reaction, and follow-up questions to respond. Student B, answer the questions with your ideas from Task A. Change roles and practice again.

Ex **A:** What did you do last weekend?
B: I went to my part-time job on Saturday and played video games with my friends on Sunday.
A: With your friends? That's nice. What kind of games did you play?

C Change your partner. This time, practice talking about each other's weekend. Try to keep the conversation going with many follow-up questions.

Ex **A:** How was your weekend?
B: It was terrible. I got up late on Sunday and dropped my phone in the toilet.
A: In the toilet? That's too bad. What did you do then?
B: I bought a new one. How about you? What did you do last weekend?
A: I ...

Weekend Events Unit 3

Short Talk ▸ Favorite weekend activities

Listening

A Listen to the hints from Mark and Alice. Then answer questions 1–3.

	Mark	Alice
1. When do they like to do it?		
2. Who do they do it with?		
3. Where do they like to do it?		
4. What are their favorite weekend activities?		

B Listen again and try to guess the answer for question 4.

Speaking

A Prepare hints about your favorite weekend activity.

- Where do you do it? _____
- Who do you do it with? _____
- When do you usually do it? _____
- How do you feel when you do it? _____
- Are there any other hints? _____

B Work in groups. Take turns to give hints. Ask questions until you can get the answer.

A Which skills from this unit were easier or more difficult for you? Make a mark on the lines.

Echo   EASY ——————— OK ——————— DIFFICULT
Reaction   EASY ——————— OK ——————— DIFFICULT
Follow-up Questions EASY ——————— OK ——————— DIFFICULT

B Write two words/expressions from this unit that you want to remember.

1. _____ 2. _____

Review of Units 1–3

Unit 1 Introductions

A Work in pairs. Take turns to look at the Seven Characters section on page 9 and ask some questions to complete the information below.

Name: Alice Canty
Hometown: _____
Major: _____
School Year: _____
Likes: _____

Name: Dan Blake
Hometown: _____
Major: _____
School Year: _____
Likes: _____

Name: Mark Franklin
Hometown: _____
Major: _____
School Year: _____
Likes: _____

Name: June Yang
Hometown: _____
Major: _____
School Year: _____
Likes: _____

B Imagine you are one of the characters from Task A. Take turns to introduce yourself and ask each other questions.

C Now, introduce yourself to your partner with your own information.

Unit 2 Daily Life

A Match each percentage to the sentence describing frequency.

100% •   • I **sometimes** forget to do my homework.
80% •   • I **hardly ever** oversleep.
70% •   • I **never** fall asleep in English class.
30% •   • I **always** watch TV at night.
10% •   • I **occasionally** go to a party.
5% •   • I **usually** stay up late on Friday.
0% •   • I **often** study in the library.

28

Review of Units 1–3

B Work in pairs. Take turns to talk about the frequency of the activities below.

How often do you ...? Do you usually ...?

- cook for your family or friends
- drink cola
- eat fruit
- go swimming
- listen to music on a CD
- play games on your phone
- read novels
- study English
- study in the library
- wake up before 8 a.m.

Unit 3 Weekend Events

Work in pairs. Take turns to talk about the events below. Use echo, reaction, and follow-up questions to respond.

- I bought a new pair of sneakers.
- I broke my phone.
- I cooked dinner for my English teacher.
- I crashed my parent's car.
- I got a new part-time job.
- I have a headache today.
- I live with my family.
- I went out with my friends last night.
- I'm going to Paris next month.
- It's my birthday tomorrow.

Combined Language Tasks

A Complete the sentences with your own ideas.

1. I was born in _____.
2. I major in _____.
3. I always _____ before I go to bed.
4. I usually _____ when I want to relax.
5. I never _____ in the morning.
6. Last night, I _____.

B Work in pairs. Take turns to tell each other your sentences from Task A. Use echo, reaction, and follow-up questions to respond. Try to keep the conversation going.

Wrap-up Which units were easier or more difficult for you? Make a mark on the lines.

Unit 1: Introductions
Unit 2: Daily Life
Unit 3: Weekend Events

29

Unit 4

Small Talk

Greeting people › Continuing a conversation

Preparation

A Write the expression matching each picture.

- I go to school by bike.
- I never forget to do my homework.
- I watched a great movie.
- I'm great.
- Nothing much.
- I met an old friend.
- I walk my dog every morning.
- I work at a restaurant.
- I'm OK.

1. _____

2. _____

3. _____

4. _____

5. _____

6. _____

7. _____

8. _____

9. _____

Small Talk Unit 4

B Complete the sentences with your own ideas.

1. [Free Time Activity]   I _____ in my free time.
2. [Part-time Job]   I work at _____.
3. [Sport]   I play _____.
4. [Movie]   I like _____.
5. [Food]   I love _____.

C Work in pairs. Student A, ask your partner the questions below. Student B, answer the questions with your ideas from Task B. Change roles and practice again.

1. What do you do in your free time?

   I … in my free time.

2. Do you have a part-time job?

   Yes, I do. I work at …

3. Do you play any sports?

   Yes, I do. I play …

4. What kind of movies do you like?

   I like …

5. What's your favorite food?

   I love …

Conversation Model

A Fill in the blanks with the words below. Then listen to the conversation and check your answers.

- are you
- do you
- do you like
- is that

Hey, Shin. How ⓐ_____ today?

I'm not bad, but a little sleepy because I work ❶ late on Mondays.

Oh. Where ⓑ_____ work?

I work at ❷ Pizza-lulu. I ❸ deliver pizzas three times a week.

Wow, ⓒ_____ hard?

Yes, but it's fun too. By the way Yolanda, ⓓ_____ ❹ Hawaiian pizza?

No, I don't. I think that ❺ pineapple on a pizza is a bad idea.

B Work in pairs. Read the conversation with your partner. Change roles once. Then practice again with the substitutions below.

[Substitution 1] ❶ every morning ❷ a coffee shop ❸ serve customers five days
❹ to drink coffee in the morning? ❺ tea is better

[Substitution 2] ❶ until midnight ❷ a movie theater ❸ make popcorn three nights
❹ going to the movies ❺ it's more fun to watch DVDs

Practice

Greeting People

[Greetings]
- Hey. How's it going?
- Hi. How are you?
- Hello. What's up?
- Hey. What's new?

[Responses]
- I'm great! • I'm pretty good. • I'm alright/OK.
- I'm not bad. • I'm not too good. • I'm terrible!
- Nothing much.
- **I got** a new girlfriend. • **I met** an old friend. • **I saw** a great movie.

Continuing a Conversation

[Reason]
A: What do you do in your free time?
B: I like to go to the park **because** I enjoy running.

[Frequency]
A: Where do you work?
B: I work at Pizza-lulu. I deliver pizzas **four times a week**.

[Opinion]
A: Do you like Hawaiian pizza?
B: No, I don't. **I think** that pineapple on a pizza is a bad idea.

[Question]
A: Do you like your job?
B: Yes, I do. By the way, **do you like** Hawaiian pizza?

 Read each question below and write a response with a reason, frequency, opinion, or question.

1. Do you like to travel?
   [Reason] _____

2. What do you do in your free time?
   [Frequency] _____

3. How do you come to school?
   [Opinion] _____

4. Who is your favorite actor?
   [Question] _____

 Work in pairs. Practice talking about the topics from Task A. Greet each other when you start the conversation. Use the expressions with a reason, frequency, opinion, and question.

Ex
A: Hi, Alice. **How's it going?**
B: **I'm OK.** How about you, June?
A: **I'm pretty good.** By the way, **do you like to travel?**
B: Yes, I do. I love traveling **because** I can meet many people. **Do you like to travel?**
A: Well, I don't like to travel very much **because** I have cats at home.

Expanded Conversation

A Complete questions 9 and 10 with your own ideas.

1. ☐ Do you have any pets?
2. ☐ What kind of music do you like?
3. ☐ Do you like karaoke?
4. ☐ What sports do you like?
5. ☐ Do you prefer tea or coffee?
6. ☐ How many people are in your family?
7. ☐ Which country would you like to visit?
8. ☐ Do you like studying English?
9. ☐ _____
10. ☐ _____

B Work in pairs. Make a small ball with a piece of paper or tissue. Student A, ask one of the questions from Task A and check the box. Student B, drop the ball in the middle of the chart below. Then answer the question with a reason, frequency, opinion, or question. Change roles and practice a few times.

Reason	Frequency
Opinion	Question

Drop a ball here!

C Change your partner. This time, greet each other when you start the conversation. First, choose one of the questions with no check from Task A. Try to continue the conversation until you finish asking all the questions.

Short Talk ▸ Part-time jobs

Listening

A Listen to the short talks by Mark and Dan. Then answer the questions.

	Mark	Dan
1. Where are their working places located?		
2. When did they start working there?		
3. How much do they earn an hour?		

B Listen again and circle the words to complete the sentences.

1. Mark [enjoys / doesn't enjoy] his job because the money [is / isn't] good and sometimes he is too [free / busy].
2. Dan [enjoys / doesn't enjoy] his job because he [can / can't] earn a lot of money and one of his coworkers is really [cute / mean].

Speaking

A Prepare for a short talk about your part-time job. If you don't have one, imagine you are working.

- I work at _____.
- I started working there _____.
- I usually work for _____ hours a week and earn _____ an hour.
- I think _____.

B Work in groups. Take turns to give a short talk.

Wrap-up

A Complete the sentence by circling one of the words.

Continuing conversations was [fun / useful / difficult].

B Write two words/expressions from this unit that you want to remember.

1. _____ 2. _____

Unit 5

Likes and Dislikes

Talking about preferences | Giving reasons

Preparation

A Write the activity matching each picture.

- cleaning the house
- going to concerts
- reading comics
- surfing the Internet
- working out
- going shopping
- playing video games
- staying at home
- watching horror movies

1. _____

2. _____

3. _____

4. _____

5. _____

6. _____

7. _____

8. _____

9. _____

Likes and Dislikes   Unit 5

B   Are the words below positive (+) or negative (–)? Write + or –.

- a waste of money ☐
- a waste of time ☐
- bad for you ☐
- boring ☐
- cheap ☐
- dangerous ☐
- difficult ☐
- easy ☐
- exciting ☐
- expensive ☐
- fun ☐
- good for you ☐
- interesting ☐
- noisy ☐
- relaxing ☐
- scary ☐
- tiring ☐
- worthwhile ☐

C   Complete the sentences with some words from Task B.

1. Reading comics is _____ and _____.
2. Going shopping is _____ and _____.
3. Cleaning the house is _____ and/but _____.
4. Watching horror movies is _____ and/but _____.

D   Work in pairs. Student A, ask your partner the questions below. Student B, answer the questions with your ideas from Task C. Change roles and practice again.

1. Do you like reading comics?
   Yes/No, it's …

2. Do you like going shopping?
   Yes/No, it's …

3. What do you think about cleaning the house?
   I think it's …

4. What do you think of watching horror movies?
   I think it's …

Conversation Model

A Fill in the blanks with the words below. Then listen to the conversation and check your answers.

- best
- boring
- day off
- doing

Hi, Mark. What are you ⓐ_____ today?

Hey, Mariko. I have the ⓑ_____, so I'm going to ❶play video games. Do you like ❷playing video games?

It's OK, but it's a little ⓒ_____. I love ❸surfing in my free time. It's the ⓓ_____. It's really ❹fun.

Really? I'm not a fan of ❸surfing. It's so ❺scary. But I have a great ❻surfing video game!

B Work in pairs. Read the conversation with your partner. Change roles once. Then practice again with the substitutions below.

[Substitution 1] ❶ watch TV ❷ watching TV ❸ working out
 ❹ good for you ❺ tiring ❻ fitness

[Substitution 2] ❶ read a comic ❷ reading comics ❸ going to concerts
 ❹ exciting ❺ noisy ❻ guitar

Likes and Dislikes — Unit 5

Practice

Asking about Preferences

- **Do you like** going to concerts?
- **What do you think about/of** reading comics?

Degree of Preferences

Like the most
1. Going hiking **is the best.**
2. _____
3. _____
4. _____
5. _____
6. _____
7. _____

Like the least
8. _____

Giving Reasons

[Stronger]
- Staying at home is **so** relaxing.
- Surfing the Internet is **really** fun.
- Working out is **such** a waste of time.

[Softer]
- Cleaning the house is **a bit** tiring.
- Going swimming is **a little** boring.
- Watching horror movies is **kind of** interesting.

 A Complete the list of Degree of Preferences with these expressions.

- Going hiking **is OK.**
- **I enjoy** going hiking.
- **I love** going hiking.
- **I'm not a fan of** going hiking.
- **I can't stand** going hiking.
- **I hate** going hiking.
- **I really like** going hiking.

B Work in pairs. Practice talking about some activities from Preparation Task A. Use the expressions for preferences above.

Ex A: **Do you like** <u>playing video games</u>?
    B: Yes, **I love** <u>playing video games</u>. **Do you like** <u>going shopping</u>?
    A: No, **I can't stand** <u>going shopping</u>. **Do you like** ...?

C Change your partner. This time, explain the reasons for your preferences with some words from Preparation Task B.

Ex A: **What do you think about** <u>playing video games</u>?
    B: **I love** <u>playing video games</u>. **It's really** <u>fun</u>! **What do you think of** <u>going shopping</u>?
    A: **I can't stand** <u>going shopping</u>. **It's so** <u>boring</u>. **What do you think of** ...?

Expanded Conversation

A Write three activities you like and three activities you dislike with the reasons.

Likes

Ex I love listening to music. It's really relaxing.

1. _____
2. _____
3. _____

Dislikes

Ex I can't stand working out. It's so tiring.

1. _____
2. _____
3. _____

B Talk to your classmates. Find three people who like the activities you like and three people who dislike the activities you dislike.

Ex A: Do you like …?
    B: Yes, … / No, …
    A: I like that too! / I don't like that either.
    B: Why? / Why not?
    A: I think it's …

Likes

1. Name: _____   We both like _____.
2. Name: _____   We both like _____.
3. Name: _____   We both like _____.

Dislikes

1. Name: _____   We both dislike _____.
2. Name: _____   We both dislike _____.
3. Name: _____   We both dislike _____.

Likes and Dislikes Unit 5

Short Talk ▸ Activities on Sunday morning

Listening

A Listen to the short talks by Shin and Alice. Then match their names to the activities.

Shin •
Alice •

- cleaning
- doing yoga
- going to concerts
- practicing bass guitar

- boring
- exciting
- relaxing
- worthwhile

B Listen again and match the activities to the words that they used.

Speaking

A Prepare for a short talk about your typical Sunday morning.

What do you often do on Sunday morning? Write two activities.

1. _____
2. _____

Do you like doing them? Why or why not?

1. _____
2. _____

B Work in groups. Take turns to give a short talk. Try to continue talking with the words "because," "and," "but," or "so."

Wrap-up

A Complete the sentence with some words from Preparation Task B.

This unit was _____ and _____.

B Write two words/expressions from this unit that you want to remember.

1. _____ 2. _____

Unit 6

Student Life

Talking about needs and wants 〉 Recommending places

Preparation

A Write the facility name matching each picture.

- bookstore
- cafeteria
- computer lab
- fitness center
- health center
- international student center
- learning assistance center
- library
- student affairs office

1. _____

2. _____

3. _____

4. _____

5. _____

6. _____

7. _____

8. _____

9. _____

Student Life Unit 6

B Which school facilities do you use for the following needs and wants? Write the picture numbers from Task A.

1. borrow books ☐
2. buy a corn dog ☐
3. buy textbooks ☐
4. exercise ☐
5. make a student ID card ☐
6. meet international students ☐
7. meet with an academic advisor ☐
8. see a school doctor ☐
9. use a computer ☐

C Complete the sentences with some facility names from Task A.

1. The best place to eat lunch is the _____.
2. The best place to take a break is the _____.
3. I often use the _____.
4. I never use the _____.

D Work in pairs. Student A, ask your partner the questions below. Student B, answer the questions with your ideas from Task C. Change roles and practice again.

1. Where is the best place to eat lunch?
   I think it's the ...

2. Where is the best place to take a break?
   I think it's the ...

3. Which school facilities do you often use?
   I often use the ...

4. Which school facilities do you never use?
   I never use the ...

43

Conversation Model

A Fill in the blanks with the words below. Then listen to the conversation and check your answers.

- across from
- do you
- fitness center
- need to

Hey, Shin. Do you want to go to the ⓐ_____ with me?

Sure! But first, I ❶need to make a new student ID card.

Oh, then you ⓑ_____ go to the ❷student affairs office.

Well, ⓒ_____ know where it is?

Yeah, it's in ❸Building 1, on the ❹first floor. It's ⓓ_____ the ❺international student center.

Thanks, Dan. ❻You are the best!

B Work in pairs. Read the conversation with your partner. Change roles once. Then practice again with the substitutions below.

[Substitution 1] ❶ need to buy a photocopy card   ❷ library   ❸ Building 2
❹ fifth   ❺ health center   ❻ That's good to know!

[Substitution 2] ❶ want to eat a corn dog   ❷ cafeteria   ❸ South Building
❹ third   ❺ bookstore   ❻ Thanks for your help!

Student Life Unit 6

Practice

Talking about Needs and Wants

[Needs]
- **I have to** make a new student ID card.
- **I need to** drink something.

[Wants]
- **I want to** eat a corn dog.
- **I'd like to** use a computer.

Asking about Places

- **Where should I go?**
- **Where is the best place** to study?
- **Do you know where it is?**

Recommending Places

- **You need to go to** the student affairs office.
- **You should visit** the learning assistance center.
- **The best place to** eat lunch **is** the cafeteria.

Describing Locations

- **It's in** Building 1.
- **It's on the** first/second/third/fourth/fifth/sixth **floor**.
- **It's next to** the convenience store.
- **It's across from** the library.
- **It's between** the supermarket **and** the bank.

A Work in pairs. Practice talking about the needs and wants from Preparation Task B. Use the questions and recommendations about places.

Ex A: **I need to** <u>see a school doctor</u>. **Where should I go?**
    B: **You should go to** <u>the health center</u>.
    A: Thanks, Mark. You are the best!

B Change your partner. This time, practice talking about school faclities and other places around North Beach University. Student A, look at page 47. Student B, look at page 48.

Expanded Conversation

Work in pairs. Look at the map of North Beach University (Building 1) and other places around the campus. Take turns recommending places and describing locations. Use one of the needs/wants below or your own idea to start a conversation.

- buy a comic book
- buy strawberries
- eat Japanese food
- get some money
- report your stolen bicycle
- buy an ice cream
- do all night karaoke
- get a boyfriend/girlfriend
- go on a date
- see a night view
- buy shoes
- do your homework
- get a part-time job
- lose weight
- take a walk

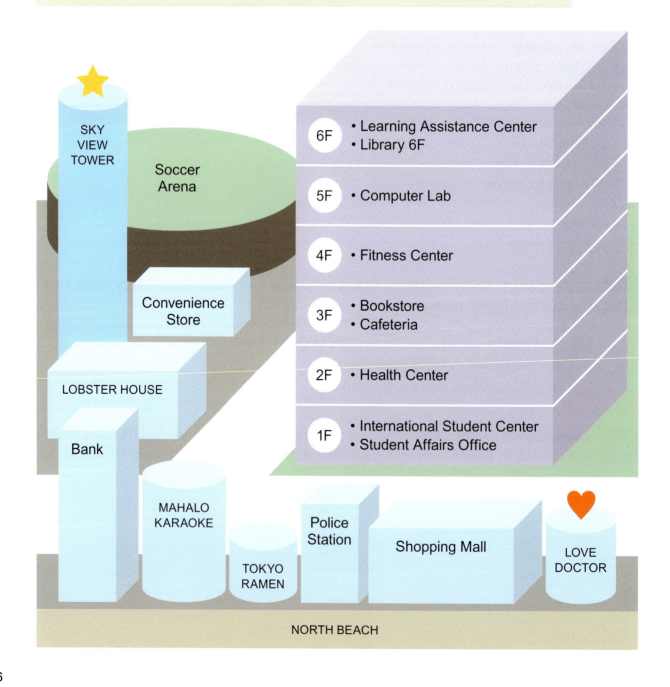

Student Life Unit 6

Student A

I You are now on the campus of North Beach University. Tell your partner your needs/wants and write the best places to go and their locations.

Ex
A: **I want to** study for a test.
B: Oh, then **you should go to** the library.
A: Well, **do you know where it is?**
B: Yeah, **it's** on the sixth floor. **It's** next to the learning assistance center.

Needs and Wants	Places	Locations
Ex study for a test	library	– on the sixth floor – next to the learning assistance center
1. join a Spanish class		
2. get some money		
3. buy a magazine		
4. get love advice		
5. hang out with friends		

II Change roles. This time, listen to your partner's needs/wants. Then recommend places and describe their locations.

Needs and Wants	Places	Locations
1. eat a lobster	Lobster House	– across from Building 1 – next to Sky View Tower
2. buy a notebook	bookstore	– on the third floor – across from the cafeteria
3. see a doctor	health center	– in Building 1 – on the second floor
4. use a computer	computer lab	– in Building 1 – on the fifth floor
5. see a beautiful view	Sky View Tower	– between Lobster House and the convenience store

47

Student B

I You are now on the campus of North Beach University. Listen to your partner's needs/wants. Then recommend places and describe their locations.

Ex A: I want to study for a test.
  B: Oh, then **you should go to** the library.
  A: Well, **do you know where it is?**
  B: Yeah, **it's** on the sixth floor. It's next to the learning assistance center.

Needs and Wants	Places	Locations
Ex study for a test	library	– on the sixth floor – next to the learning assistance center
1. join a Spanish class	student affairs office	– in Building 1 – on the first floor
2. get some money	bank	– across from Building 1 – next to Lobster House
3. buy a magazine	shopping mall	– between Love Doctor and the police station
4. get love advice	Love Doctor	– across from Building 1 – next to the shopping mall
5. hang out with friends	Mahalo Karaoke	– between Tokyo Ramen and the bank

II Change roles. This time, tell your partner your needs/wants and write the best places to go and their locations.

Needs and Wants	Places	Locations
1. eat a lobster		
2. buy a notebook		
3. see a doctor		
4. use a computer		
5. see a beautiful view		

Student Life Unit 6

Short Talk ▸ Today's events

Listening

A Listen to the short talks by Mariko and Mark. Then cross out the places they don't visit. 🎧 25–26

Mariko
- ☐ cafeteria
- ☐ fitness center
- ☐ international student center
- ☐ library
- ☐ Lobster House
- ☐ student affairs office

Mark
- ☐ bookstore
- ☐ convenience store
- ☐ fitness center
- ☐ health center
- ☐ learning assistance center
- ☐ soccer arena

B Listen again and put numbers in the order of the places they visit. 🎧 25–26

Speaking

A Imagine you are a student at North Beach University. Prepare for a short talk about your needs and wants for today. Look at the map on page 46 for some ideas.

- What did you already do this morning? _____

- What do you have to do this afternoon? _____

- What do you want to do tonight? _____

B Work in groups. Take turns to give a short talk.

Wrap-up

A Where is the best place to practice English in your school?
_____

B Write two words/expressions from this unit that you want to remember.

1. _____ 2. _____

Review of Units 4–6

Unit 4 — Small Talk

A Work in pairs. Take turns to ask and answer the questions below. Try to continue the conversation with a reason, frequency, opinion, or question.

- Do you like American music?
- What kind of movies do you like?
- How often do you play sports?
- What's your favorite food?

B Complete the questions with your own ideas.

1. Do you have _____?
2. Do you like _____?
3. How often do you _____?
4. What kind of _____ do you like?
5. What's your favorite _____?
6. Where do you like to _____?

C Change your partner. Make a small ball with a piece of paper or tissue. Student A, ask one of the questions from Task B. Student B, look at page 34, drop the ball in the middle of the chart, and answer the question. Change roles and practice a few times.

Unit 5 — Likes and Dislikes

A Circle some words in the wrong category. Then look at Preparation Task B on page 37 to check your answers.

Positive			Negative		
a waste of time	boring	difficult	a waste of money	bad for you	cheap
exciting	expensive	good for you	dangerous	easy	fun
interesting	relaxing	worthwhile	noisy	scary	tiring

50

Review of Units 4–6

B Work in pairs. Take turns to talk about your preferences for the activities below. Use some words from Task A to explain the reasons.

- cooking dinner
- going camping
- going shopping
- going swimming
- playing games on your phone
- playing video games
- studying English
- travelling by train
- watching horror movies

Unit 6 Student Life

Work in pairs. Student A, choose one of the needs/wants below and ask your partner where to go. Student B, recommend the best place in/near your school. Chnage roles and practice a few times.

- eat an inexpensive lunch
- eat a delicious lunch
- eat noodles for lunch
- find out about study abroad programs
- make a student ID card
- practice playing the guitar
- practice speaking English
- practice yoga
- prepare a presentation
- relax after school
- study for a test
- use a photocopier

Combined Language Tasks

You are now on the campus of North Beach University. Take turns to talk about a place on the map on page 46. Use the words/expressions from Units 4–6 to keep the conversation going.

- Do you know …?
- Do you like …?
- How often do you …?
- What's your favorite …?
- Where do you like to …?
- Where is the best place to …?

Ex
A: **Do you like** to eat at Lobster House?
B: Yes, I always eat lunch there. **I think** Lobster House **is the best**!
A: Really? **I love** eating lunch on the beach. I eat there twice a week. …

Wrap-up

Which units were easier or more difficult for you? Make a mark on the lines.

Unit 4: Small Talk
Unit 5: Likes and Dislikes
Unit 6: Student Life

EASY ——— OK ——— DIFFICULT

Unit 7 Family

Describing appearance | Talking about similarity

Preparation

A Choose figures matching the words for height and body type. The answer can be more than one.

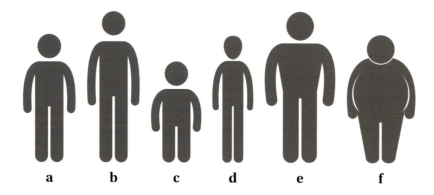

a   b   c   d   e   f

1. short: _____
2. average height: _____
3. tall: _____
4. slim: _____
5. average build: _____
6. muscular: _____
7. overweight: _____

B Read the information below and look at the words for hair and facial features. Look up new words in a dictionary.

The verbs to describe hair and facial features are "is/have/has/wear(s)."
- My hair **is** curly and brown. / Her hair **is** blonde. / He **is** bald.
- I **have** curly brown hair. / She **has** dark skin. / He **has** a mustache.
- They **wear** glasses. / He **wears** glasses.

The description order for hair is "length>type>color."
- He has **short straight black** hair.

Hair

[Length]	[Type]	[Color]	[Others]
short	straight	black	balding
medium	wavy	brown	bald
shoulder-length	curly	blonde	
long		red	
		grey	

Facial Features

[Skin Color]	[Others]
light	glasses
tanned	mustache
dark	beard
	clean-shaven

Family Unit 7

C Complete the descriptions with the words from Task B. Do not use the same word twice.

Sandra
She has _____ _____ _____ hair and _____ skin.

Jim
He is _____. He has _____ hair and a _____.

Antonio
He is _____. He wears _____ and has a _____.

Naomi
She has _____ _____ _____ hair and _____ skin.

D Work in pairs. Student A, ask your partner the questions below. Student B, answer the questions with your descriptions from Task C. Change roles and practice again. Check if you have the same answers.

1. What does Sandra look like?
   She has …

2. What does Jim look like?
   He is …

3. What does Antonio look like?
   He is …

4. What does Naomi look like?
   She has …

53

Conversation Model

A Fill in the blanks with the words below. Then listen to the conversation and check your answers.

- short
- sisters
- slim
- younger

Do you have any brothers or ⓐ_____, Shin?

Yeah, I have a ⓑ_____ brother.

What does he look like?

He is tall and ⓒ_____. He has dark brown eyes and ⓓ_____ straight black hair. How about you?

I have a younger sister and ❶ an older brother.

What does your brother look like?

My brother is ❷ very tall and has ❸ straight brown hair and ❹ green eyes. He looks ❺ nothing like me!

B Work in pairs. Read the conversation with your partner. Change roles once. Then practice again with the substitutions below.

[Substitution 1] ❶ a twin ❷ average height ❸ wavy red ❹ blue ❺ just

[Substitution 2] ❶ a younger ❷ slim ❸ short blonde ❹ blue ❺ a bit

Family Unit 7

Practice

Talking about Family Members

- **Do you have** any brothers or sisters?
- **What does** your father **look like?**
- **Does** your mother **look like you?**

- **No, I don't.** I'm an only child.
- **Yes, I do. I have** a younger sister and an older brother.
- My father is tall and slim.
- She looks nothing like me.

Descriptions

[Hair]
1. He _____ short straight black hair.
2. She _____ curly brown hair.
3. Her hair _____ curly and brown.

[Facial Features]
1. He _____ a mustache.
2. He _____ bald.
3. She _____ dark skin.
4. She _____ glasses.

[Age]
1. He _____ young/middle-aged/old.
2. He _____ a teenager.
3. She _____ in her 20s/30s/40s/50s/60s.

Similarity

Same
↕
Different

- He looks **just like** me.
- She looks **a lot like** me.
- He looks **a bit like** me.
- She looks **nothing like** me.

A Complete the list of Descriptions with the verbs "is/has/wears."

B Work in pairs. Practice talking about family members. If you are an only child, you can talk about a parent or relative.

> Ex
> A: **Do you have** any brothers or sisters?
> B: **Yes, I do. I have** an older brother and an older sister.
> A: **What does** your sister **look like?**
> B: My sister is average height and slim. She has dark eyes and long wavy brown hair.
> A: **Does** she **look like you?**
> B: She looks **a bit like** me.

C Change your partner. This time, practice describing people on the pictures. Students A and B have different information on pages 57 and 58. Student A, choose one person from the list and ask your partner the question. Student B, tell your partner the information you have. Then write the name matching the picture. Change roles until you find out all of their names.

Expanded Conversation

A Work in pairs. Take turns to describe a friend or a celebrity for your partner to draw a picture. Talk about the person's height, body type, hair, facial features, and age. Ask questions for more information to draw a picture.

Score ☐   Score ☐

B Look at each other's drawing and score it.

> 3 — The drawing looks just like him/her.
> 2 — The drawing looks a lot like him/her.
> 1 — The drawing looks a little like him/her.
> 0 — The drawing looks nothing like him/her.

C Change your partner and practice again.

Family Unit 7

Student A

Ex **A:** What do you know about <u>Antonio</u>?
B: Well, <u>Antonio</u> **has a beard** and <u>he</u> **is in his 40s**. What do you know about <u>him</u>?
A: <u>He</u> **is bald** and **wears glasses**.
B: OK, I think <u>the picture number 1</u> must be <u>Antonio</u>.
A: I think so too.

☑ **Antonio:** bald / glasses		☐ **Anna:** straight hair / slim
☐ **Daniela:** overweight / dark brown hair		☐ **Darren:** a little overweight / in his 30s
☐ **Hans:** slim / straight hair / in his 20s		☐ **Kevin:** in his 20s / glasses
☐ **Mari:** curly hair / tanned		☐ **Max:** long hair / clean-shaven
☐ **Mei:** glasses / light skin / long hair		☐ **Samantha:** blonde hair / light skin
☐ **Stacy:** shoulder-length hair / in her 20s		☐ **Steve:** clean-shaven / dark skin / glasses

1. <u>Antonio</u>   **2.** _____   **3.** _____   **4.** _____

5. _____   **6.** _____   **7.** _____   **8.** _____

9. _____   **10.** _____   **11.** _____   **12.** _____

Student B

Ex **A:** What do you know about <u>Antonio</u>?
B: Well, <u>Antonio</u> **has a beard** and <u>he</u> **is in his 40s**. What do you know about <u>him</u>?
A: <u>He</u> **is bald** and **wears glasses**.
B: OK, I think <u>the picture number 1</u> must be <u>Antonio</u>.
A: I think so too.

- ☑ **Antonio:** beard / in his 40s
- ☐ **Daniella:** long wavy hair / in her 20s
- ☐ **Hans:** long hair / glasses
- ☐ **Mari:** shoulder-length black hair
- ☐ **Mei:** straight dark brown hair / in her 20s
- ☐ **Stacy:** curly brown hair / dark skin
- ☐ **Anna:** long black hair / tanned
- ☐ **Darren:** medium dark brown hair / beard
- ☐ **Kevin:** mustache / short hair
- ☐ **Max:** straight blonde hair / light skin
- ☐ **Samantha:** slim / short hair
- ☐ **Steve:** balding / in his 40s

1. <u>Antonio</u>

2. _____

3. _____

4. _____

5. _____

6. _____

7. _____

8. _____

9. _____

10. _____

11. _____

12. _____

Family Unit 7

Short Talk ▸ Future image

Listening

A Listen to the short talks by Mark and June. Then circle the correct answers.

	Mark	Who does he look like?	a. His mother b. His father
	June	Do her mother and grandmother look alike?	a. Yes, they do. b. No, they don't.

B Listen again and circle the words to complete the sentences.

1. Mark wants to look like his [father / grandfather].
2. June doesn't want to [get shorter / have grey hair].

Speaking

A Prepare for a short talk about your own future image.

[Similarity] I will look like _____ when I'm _____ years old.
[Height]   I will be _____.
[Body Type] I will be _____.
[Hair]   _____
[Clothes]   I will wear _____.
[Hopes]   I hope I _____.

B Work in groups. Take turns to give a short talk.

Wrap-up

A Which part of this unit was most challenging for you? Circle one or two.
[Preparation / Conversation Model / Practice / Expanded Conversation / Short Talk]

B Write two words/expressions from this unit that you want to remember.
1. _____ 2. _____

59

Unit 8

Friends
Talking about personality | Giving examples

Preparation

A Look at the words to describe personality. Check the boxes if you know the meanings. Look up new words in a dictionary.

- ☐ artistic
- ☐ easygoing
- ☐ energetic
- ☐ forgetful
- ☐ friendly
- ☐ funny
- ☐ generous
- ☐ hardworking
- ☐ kind
- ☐ lazy
- ☐ moody
- ☐ noisy
- ☐ optimistic
- ☐ quiet
- ☐ reliable
- ☐ serious
- ☐ shy
- ☐ sociable
- ☐ stingy
- ☐ unique

B Choose an example personality matching each word.

1. artistic: _____
2. easygoing: _____
3. energetic: _____
4. forgetful: _____
5. funny: _____
6. generous: _____
7. lazy: _____
8. optimistic: _____
9. shy: _____
10. sociable: _____

a — always positive
b — doesn't do their homework
c — doesn't like speaking in front of people
d — gives you chocolate
e — is good at telling jokes
f — likes drawing pictures
g — loves to meet new people
h — never gets angry
i — often forgets something important
j — very active or sporty

Friends Unit 8

C Complete the sentences with some words from Task A.

1. One of my friends from high school is _____.

2. One of my classmates is _____.

3. I want to be friends with people who are _____
_____.

4. I don't want to be friends with people who are _____
_____.

D Work in pairs. Student A, ask your partner the questions below. Student B, answer the questions with your ideas from Task C. Change roles and practice again.

1.
> Tell me about one of your friends from high school.

>> He/She is …

2.
> What's one of your classmates like?

>> He/She is …

3.
> What kind of people do you want to be friends with?

>> I want to be friends with people who are …

4.
> What kind of people don't you want to be friends with?

>> I don't want to be friends with people who are …

Conversation Model

A Fill in the blanks with the words below. Then listen to the conversation and check your answers.

- lazy
- like
- remind
- sounds

Wow, you really love cats, don't you? You ⓐ_____ me of Rina.

Rina? Who is Rina? She's my ❶ best friend.

Your ❶ best friend? What's she ⓑ_____?

Well, she loves cats too. She is also ❷ energetic and really ❸ outgoing.

She ⓒ_____ ❹ active.

Yeah, she's really ❹ active. For example, she loves ❺ hiking and running. Like, she always ❻ goes for a run before school.

Wow. Now I feel ⓓ_____!

B Work in pairs. Read the conversation with your partner. Change roles once. Then practice again with the substitutions below.

[Substitution 1]	❶ roommate	❷ creative	❸ unique
	❹ artistic	❺ drawing and painting	❻ makes art for our apartment
[Substitution 2]	❶ friend from work	❷ funny	❸ sociable
	❹ outgoing	❺ to meet new people	❻ makes new friends

Friends Unit 8

Practice

Asking about People

- **What's** your best friend **like**?   ■ **Tell me about** your roommate.   ■ **Why do you think** she is lazy?

Words to Describe Personality

[Positive]				[Neutral]	[Negative]	
■ artistic	■ easygoing	■ energetic	■ friendly	■ quiet	■ forgetful	■ lazy
■ funny	■ generous	■ hardworking	■ kind	■ serious	■ moody	■ noisy
■ optimistic	■ reliable	■ sociable	■ unique	■ shy	■ stingy	

Describing Personality with Examples

- She is **really** active. **For example,** she goes jogging every morning.
- She is **kind of** artistic. She **loves** making her own clothes.
- He is **a bit** serious. **Like,** he **always** reads the newspaper.

 A What do you think about your own personality? Choose three words from Preparation Task A to complete the sentence.

I think I am _____, _____, and _____.

 B Work in pairs. Try to guess the words your partner chose. Tell your partner the words you chose, ask questions, and give examples.

> **Ex** **A:** What do you think I wrote?
> **B:** I think you wrote <u>active</u>, <u>optimistic</u>, and <u>friendly</u>.
> **A:** You got two correct! I wrote <u>optimistic</u>, <u>friendly</u>, and <u>lazy</u>.
> **B:** Why do you think you are <u>lazy</u>?
> **A:** Well, for example, I ...

Expanded Conversation

 A Work in pairs. Ask your partner about his/her best friend.

> **Ex** **A:** What's your best friend like?
> **B:** She's kind of quiet.
> **A:** Oh, really? Why do you think she is quiet?
> **B:** Like, she always reads comics in her room.

63

B This time, ask your partner about the people below.

1. old friend
2. favorite teacher
3. least favorite teacher

C Choose one of the pictures from page 57 or 58 in Unit 7 and write his/her name below. Imagine he/she is your new roommate and write the personality and examples with your own ideas.

	Roommate's Name	Personality	Examples
Ex	Kevin	– really kind – reliable – unique	– makes dinner for me – always on time – wears interesting clothes
You			
Partner 1			
Partner 2			

D Work in pairs. Ask your partner about his/her roommate from Task C and write the information in the columns for Partner 1.

Ex A: What's your new roommate's name?
B: His name is Kevin.
A: What's he like?
B: Well, he is really kind, reliable, and unique.
A: Why do you think he is unique?
B: Like, he always wears interesting clothes.

E Change your partner. Repeat Task D and write the information in the columns for Partner 2.

Friends Unit 8

Short Talk ▸ Individual personality

Listening

A Listen to the short talks by Dan and Alice. Then circle the words to complete the sentences. 🎧 33-34

Dan	His best friend Jonathan [loves / doesn't like] meeting new people. He [sometimes / never] oversleeps and misses his classes.
Alice	Her best friend Anna plays the [guitar / piano] and wants to be a famous musician. She [sometimes / never] forgets a promise.

B Listen again and guess the missing parts. Then complete the sentences with the words to describe their individual personality. 🎧 33-34

1. Jonathan is _____ and _____.
2. Anna is _____ and _____.

Speaking

A Prepare for a short talk about your personality.

[Good Points]   A good point about my personality is that I'm _____.
                I always _____.
[Weak Points]   My weak point is that I'm _____.
                I'm not very _____.
[Opinion]   I'd like to be more _____.

B Work in groups. Take turns to give a short talk. Try to give examples about your good points and weak points.

Wrap-up

A What kind of people are good at studying English? Complete the sentence with a word from Preparation Task A.

_____ people are good at studying English.

B Write two words/expressions from this unit that you want to remember.

1. _____   2. _____

Unit 9: Going Out

Talking about free time | Arranging schedules

Preparation

A Write the words in the columns to make correct expressions. Some words can be used more than once.

- a basketball game
- a date
- a drink
- a live concert
- at my house
- coffee
- dancing
- shopping
- snowboarding
- the beach
- the park
- with my friends

Go	Go to	Go on
bowling	a donut shop	a trip

Go for	Play	Hang out
dinner	video games	in town

B Complete the sentences with some activities from Task A.

1. I usually _____ with my friends.
2. I occasionally _____ with my friends.
3. I never _____ with my friends.
4. I like to hang out with my friends in _____.
5. If I go on a date, I want to _____.

66

C Work in pairs. Student A, ask your partner the questions below. Student B, answer the questions with your ideas from Task B. Change roles and practice again.

1. Which activities do you usually do with your friends?

   I usually ... with my friends.

2. Which activities do you occasionally do with your friends?

   I occasionally ... with my friends.

3. Which activities do you never do with your friends?

   I never ... with my friends.

4. Where do you like to hang out with your friends?

   I like to hang out with my friends in ...

5. If you go on a date, what do you want to do?

   If I go on a date, I want to ...

Conversation Model

A Fill in the blanks with the words below. Then listen to the conversation and check your answers.

- forward
- meet
- nice idea
- together

Alice. Long time no see. Let's get ⓐ _____ ❶ on Saturday.

OK, I'm free. How about ❷ going shopping?

Yeah. Where shall we go?

That's a ⓑ _____. Then we could go for ❸ lunch if you like.

We could go to ❹ Rivertown.

Sounds good. Why don't we ⓒ _____ at 10 a.m.?

Sorry, but 10 a.m. is no good for me.

OK, how about ❺ 11:00?

❻ Perfect. So, let's meet at the bus stop at ❺ 11:00.

Great. I'm looking ⓓ _____ to it!

B Work in pairs. Read the conversation with your partner. Change roles once. Then practice again with the substitutions below.

| [Substitution 1] | ❶ tomorrow | ❷ going to the beach | ❸ a drink |
| | ❹ White Sand Beach | ❺ noon | ❻ OK. |

| [Substitution 2] | ❶ next Friday | ❷ watching a movie | ❸ pizza |
| | ❹ Sunshine Tower | ❺ 10:30 | ❻ No problem. |

Going Out Unit 9

Practice

Talking about Free Time

[Invitation]
- **Are you free** on Tuesday?
- **How about** going shopping?
- **Why don't we** do something on Friday?
- **Why don't we** go for a drive?
- **We could** go for lunch **if you like**.

[Responses]
- Yes, **I'm free**. • **That's a nice idea**.
- **Sounds good**. • **OK, that sounds like fun**.
- **Nice idea, but** it's too expensive.
- **Sorry, but** 10 a.m. **is no good for me**.

Arranging Schedules

[Time] • What time shall we meet? • **How about** 6 p.m.? • **Let's meet at** 10 a.m.

[Place] • Where shall we go? • Where shall we meet? • **Let's meet at** the station.

[Closing] • OK, that's 2 p.m. on Sunday, in Rivertown, **right**? • Great. I'm looking forward to it.
• So, **let's meet at** the bus stop **at** 11:00.

 A Work in pairs. Practice talking about free time and arranging schedules. Use some expressions from Preparation Task A and the list above.

 Ex
A: Long time no see. **Are you free on** ...?
B: Yes, **I'm free**.
A: **Let's** ...
B: **Nice idea, but** ...
A: OK, **why don't we** ...?
B: **Sounds good. What time shall we meet?**
A: **How about** ...?
B: Great. Where shall we meet?
A: **Let's meet at** ...
B: OK, **great**.

 B Change your partner. Student A, look at your schedule below and ask your partner about his/her free time. Then invite him/her to do two activities from the list. Student B, look at your schedule on page 70 and respond to the invitation. Change roles and practice again.

 Ex
A: Hi, Dan. **Let's get together** on Friday afternoon.
B: **Sorry, but** Friday afternoon **is no good for me**.
A: OK. **How about** Thursday afternoon?
B: Yes, **I'm free**.
A: OK, **why don't we** ...?

Student A

[Schedule]

	Mon	Tue	Wed	Thu	Fri	Sat	Sun
Morning	○	○	×	×	○	○	×
Afternoon	×	○	×	○	○	×	○

[Activities]
- Catch a movie
- Go dancing
- Go for a drive
- Go to a live concert
- Go to an amusement park

69

Student B

[Schedule]

	Mon	Tue	Wed	Thu	Fri	Sat	Sun
Morning	O	×	O	×	O	×	O
Afternoon	O	O	×	O	×	×	O

[Activities]
- Go out for dinner
- Go snowboarding
- Have a barbeque
- Have a house party
- Play basketball

Expanded Conversation

 A Complete the days of week on the left of the calendar. Then think of five activities/events that you have planned this week and write them down. Don't forget to include the time.

	Morning	Afternoon	Night
_____day (Today)			
_____day			
_____day			
_____day			
_____day			
_____day			
_____day			

B Work in pairs. Ask your partner about his/her schedule and make some plans together. Then write them down on the calendar.

Going Out Unit 9

Short Talk ▸ A favorite place to go with friends

Listening

A Listen to the short talks by Mariko and Shin. Then answer questions 1 and 2.

	Mariko	Shin
1. Where do they like to go?		
2. How often do they go?		
3. When do they go there?	a. Around noon b. Early in the morning	a. In the afternoon b. In the evening
4. What do they like to do afterwards?	a. Go for a drive b. Go for lunch	a. Study b. Watch a movie

B Listen again and circle the correct answers for questions 3 and 4.

Speaking

A Prepare for a short talk about your favorite place to go with your friends.

- Where do you like to go with your friends? _____
- How often do you go there? _____
- What can you do there? _____
- What do you like about it? _____

B Work in groups. Take turns to give a short talk.

Wrap-up

A Which part of this unit was most fun for you? Circle one or two.
[Preparation / Conversation Model / Practice / Expanded Conversation / Short Talk]

B Write two words/expressions from this unit that you want to remember.
1. _____ 2. _____

71

Review of Units 7–9

Unit 7 | Family

A Draw one of your family members or relatives and write his/her name, age, and description.

[Name] _____
[Age] _____
[Body Type] _____
[Hair] _____
[Facial Features] _____

B Work in pairs. Take turns to describe your family member or relative for your partner to draw. Ask questions for more information to draw them.

C Look at your partner's drawing. Is it similar to your drawing?

Unit 8 | Friends

A Look at the words to describe personality and write + (positive), – (negative), or 0 (neutral). Then look at the list on page 63 to check your answers.

- artistic ☐
- friendly ☐
- kind ☐
- optimistic ☐
- shy ☐

- easygoing ☐
- funny ☐
- lazy ☐
- quiet ☐
- sociable ☐

- energetic ☐
- generous ☐
- moody ☐
- reliable ☐
- stingy ☐

- forgetful ☐
- hardworking ☐
- noisy ☐
- serious ☐
- unique ☐

Review of Units 7–9

B Think of people below and write their personality with the words from Task A.

	Your Best Male Friend	Your Best Female Friend
Good Points		
Weak Points		

C Work in pairs. Take turns to talk about the two poeple from Task B. Try to give examples about their good points and weak points.

Unit 9 Going Out

A Check three activities you are interested in.

B Work in pairs. Ask your partner about his/her free time and arrange a plan for the activities both of you are interested in. Make notes of the meeting time and place.

Activities	Meeting Time	Meeting Place
☐ Eat Thai food		
☐ Go to a dinosaur museum		
☐ Go to a family restaurant		
☐ Go to a hot spring		
☐ Go to Hungry Shark Beach		
☐ Watch a horror movie		

Combined Language Tasks

A Work in a group of three or four. Each member should choose a celebrity or anime character and take turns to describe his/her appearance. Does the person look similar to anyone in your group?

B Now, take turns to describe his/her personality. Try to give examples about his/her good points and weak points.

C Imagine you are the celebrity or anime character you chose in Task A. Make a plan to go out with your group members, and arrange the meeting time and place.

Wrap-up Which units were easier or more difficult for you? Make a mark on the lines.

Unit 7: Family   EASY ——————— OK ——————— DIFFICULT
Unit 8: Friends   EASY ——————— OK ——————— DIFFICULT
Unit 9: Going Out   EASY ——————— OK ——————— DIFFICULT

Unit 10

Restaurants

Ordering food and drinks › Talking about problems

Preparation

A Write the expressions matching each picture.

- Excuse me!
- I think you forgot my order.
- My French fries are too salty.
- My pizza is cold.
- There's a spider in my salad!
- I ordered a juice, not a coffee.
- My bowl is dirty.
- My pasta tastes bad.
- There's a hair on my cake!

1. _____

2. _____

3. _____

4. _____

5. _____

6. _____

7. _____

8. _____

9. _____

Restaurants Unit 10

B Make a menu for your own restaurant.

Restaurant's Name:

Main Dishes

- _____ $_____
- _____ $_____
- _____ $_____
- _____ $_____
- _____ $_____

Drinks

- _____
  $_____
- _____
  $_____
- _____
  $_____

Dessert

- _____
  $_____
- _____
  $_____
- _____
  $_____

C Work in pairs. Student A, ask your partner the questions below. Student B, answer the questions with your own ideas. Change roles and practice again.

1. What is your favorite restaurant?

   My favorite restaurant is …

2. How often do you go there?

   I go there …

3. What do you usually order?

   I usually order …

Conversation Model

A Fill in the blanks with the words below. Then listen to the conversation and check your answers.

- everything
- immediately
- order
- right

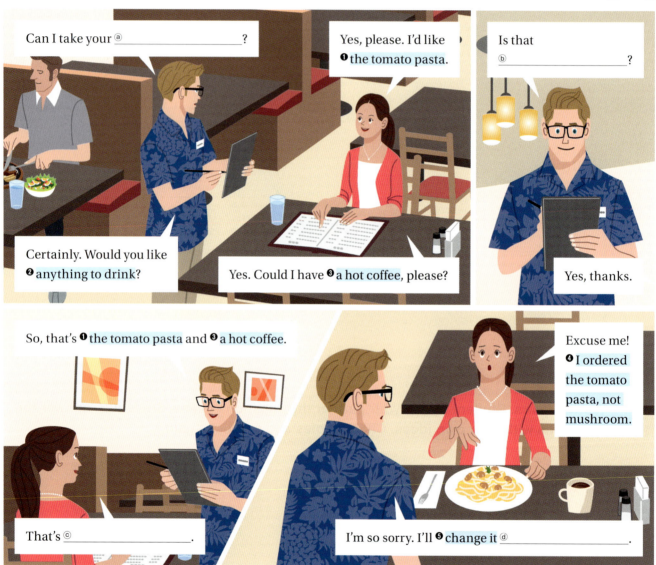

Can I take your ⓐ_____?

Yes, please. I'd like ❶ the tomato pasta.

Is that ⓑ_____?

Certainly. Would you like ❷ anything to drink?

Yes. Could I have ❸ a hot coffee, please?

Yes, thanks.

So, that's ❶ the tomato pasta and ❸ a hot coffee.

Excuse me! ❹ I ordered the tomato pasta, not mushroom.

That's ⓒ_____.

I'm so sorry. I'll ❺ change it ⓓ_____.

B Work in pairs. Read the conversation with your partner. Change roles once. Then practice again with the substitutions below.

[Substitution 1]   ❶ the grilled vegetable pizza   ❷ any dessert   ❸ the avocado ice cream
❹ My spoon is dirty.   ❺ take care of it

[Substitution 2]   ❶ the grilled salmon   ❷ anything for dessert   ❸ the cheese cake
❹ There's a spider in my salad.   ❺ bring a new one

Restaurants Unit 10

Practice

Ordering Food and Drinks

[Staff Expressions]
- **Are you ready to order?** **Can I take your order?**
- **Would you like anything to** drink?
- **Would you like anything for** dessert?
- **Would you like any** dessert?
- **Anything else?** **Is that everything?**
- **So, that's** the grilled chicken **and** the vanilla ice cream.

[Customer Expressions]
- **I'd like** the vegetable pizza.
- **I'll have** the cheesecake**, please.**
- **Could I have** an iced tea**, please?**
- **That's all. Thanks.**

Talking about Problems

[Customer Complaints]
- **I ordered** the garlic bread**, not** French fries.
- **I think you forgot** my coffee.
- **There's** a bug **on** my plate.   **There's** a hair **in** my soup.
- **My** table **is dirty.**   **My** chicken **is raw.**   **My** soup **is cold.**
- **This** curry **is too spicy.**   **This** pasta **is too salty.**
- **This** pizza **is burned.**   **These** mushrooms **are not fresh.**

[Staff Responses]
- **I'm sorry about that.**
- **I'm so sorry.**
- **I'm terribly sorry.**
- **I'll take care of it** right away.
- **I'll change it** immediately.
- **I'll bring a new one** now.

A Work in pairs. Student A, you are the staff member in a restaurant. Take care of your customer politely. Student B, you are the customer. Look at the information below and order your food and a drink. Then complain about two problems.

[Order] ▪ pasta in mushroom sauce ▪ French fries ▪ mineral water
[Problems] ▪ There's a hair on your pasta. ▪ Your French fries are salty.

Ex S: **Are you ready to order?**
C: Yes, **I'll have** the grilled chicken.
S: Certainly. **Would you like anything to** drink?
C: Yes. **Could I have** an iced tea**, please?**
S: **Anything else?**
C: No, **that's all. Thanks.**
S: **So, that's** the grilled chicken **and** an iced tea.
C: **That's right.**

C: Excuse me! **I ordered** the grilled chicken**, not** pork.
S: **I'm so sorry. I'll change it** right away.
C: And **my** fork **is dirty.**
S: **I'm terribly sorry. I'll bring a new one** immediately.

77

B Change roles. This time, Student A is the customer and Student B is the staff member.

[Order]   ■ grilled vegetable pizza   ■ avocado salad   ■ iced coffee
[Problems]   ■ Your pizza is overcooked.   ■ The staff serves you a hot coffee.

Expanded Conversation

 A Work in pairs. Take turns to be the staff member and the customer. When you take the customer's role, order three items. Then complain about two problems.

Laurenzo's Vegetarian Italian Restaurant

Menu

Main Dishes

Pasta in Tomato Sauce	$6.00
Pasta in Mushroom Sauce	$6.00
Hawaiian Style Tofu Burger	$8.00
Grilled Vegetable Pizza	$5.50

Side Dishes

Tomato Salad	$3.50
Avocado Salad	$4.50
Garlic Bread	$3.00
Vegetable Fries	$2.50

Drinks

Mineral Water	$1.50
Fresh Orange Juice	$3.00
Hot/Iced Coffee	$2.50
Hot/Iced Tea	$2.50

Dessert

Cheese Cake	$3.00
Chocolate Cake	$3.00
Ice Cream (Vanilla/Avocado/Broccoli)	$2.50

B Change your partner. This time, use the menus you made in Preparation Task B. Look at your partner's menu and order three items. Then complain about two problems.

Restaurants Unit 10

Short Talk ▸ The last restaurant I went to

Listening

A Listen to the short talks by Alice and Dan. Then answer questions 1–3. 🎧 41/42

	Alice	Dan
1. How were the prices?		
2. Was the restaurant busy?		
3. Was the food delicious?		
4. Will they go there again?		

B Listen again and try to guess the answer for question 4. 🎧 41/42

Speaking

A Prepare for a short talk about the last restaurant you went to.

- What kind of restaurant was it?
- Have you been there before?
- What did you order?
- How were the prices?
- Will you go there again?
- What food or a drink do you recommend?

B Work in groups. Take turns to give a short talk. Ask your classmates some questions about the restaurants.

Wrap-up

A Do you think you can do the following things in English in a restaurant?

1. Ordering food and a drink — YES — MAYBE — NO
2. Complaining about some problems — YES — MAYBE — NO

B Write two words/expressions from this unit that you want to remember.

1. _____ 2. _____

79

Unit 11

Shopping

Talking about shopping places | Responding to suggestions

Preparation

A Match the items to the pictures and the store type. Then write the names of your favorite stores.

Items	Pictures	Store Type	Favorite Stores
Ex. a box of chocolates	b	chocolate shop	Codiva
1. a camera			
2. a pair of jeans			
3. a pair of sneakers			
4. a pen case			
5. a suit			
6. a table lamp			
7. a wallet			

- ~~chocolate shop~~
- clothing store
- electronics store
- furniture store
- leather goods store
- shoe store
- stationery shop
- tailor

80

B

Some stores have good points and bad points. Match each expression to one with an opposite meaning.

[Good Points]

It's close by and convenient.

It's really popular.

Their designs are cool.

They have a lot of choices.

They have lots of bargains.

[Bad Points]

- It's a bit overpriced.
- It's gone out of style.
- It's far away and inconvenient.
- Their designs are boring.
- There isn't much to choose from.

C

Reorder the words to complete the conversation.

A: I want to buy a new watch. Where _____? { recommend / you / do }

B: How about the shopping mall?

A: Nice idea. Which _____? { should / I / to / store / go }

B: The _____ Time Zone. { be / best / place / would } Their watches are really cool.

A: Sounds nice! I _____. { a / give / it / try / will }

D

Work in pairs. Student A, ask your partner about three items from Task A. Student B, answer the questions with your ideas from Task A. Change roles and practice again.

1. Where would you go to buy ...?

   I'd go to ...

2. Where would you go to buy ...?

   I'd go to ...

3. Where would you go to buy ...?

   I'd go to ...

Conversation Model

A Fill in the blanks with the words below. Then listen to the conversation and check your answers.

- close by
- really popular
- recommend
- sounds great

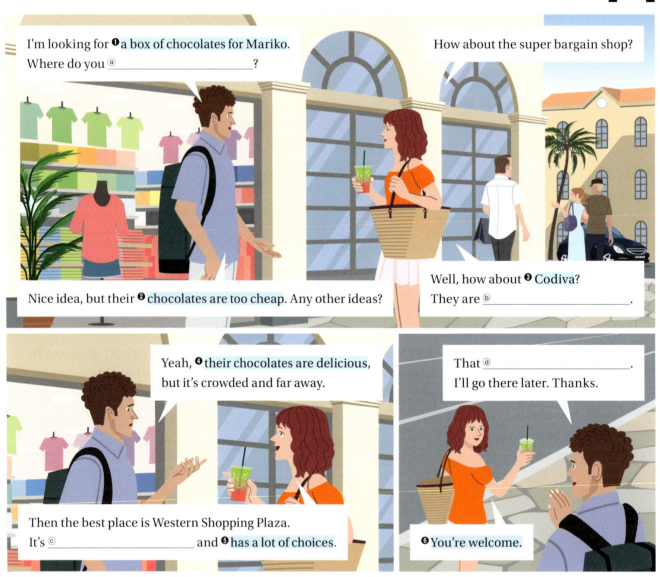

I'm looking for ❶ a box of chocolates for Mariko. Where do you ⓐ_____?

How about the super bargain shop?

Nice idea, but their ❷ chocolates are too cheap. Any other ideas?

Well, how about ❸ Codiva? They are ⓑ_____.

Yeah, ❹ their chocolates are delicious, but it's crowded and far away.

That ⓓ_____. I'll go there later. Thanks.

Then the best place is Western Shopping Plaza. It's ⓒ_____ and ❺ has a lot of choices.

❻ You're welcome.

B Work in pairs. Read the conversation with your partner. Change roles once. Then practice again with the substitutions below.

[Substitution 1] ❶ a pencil case   ❷ designs are boring   ❸ Stationary Station
❹ their designs are cool   ❺ the prices are reasonable   ❻ Anytime.

[Substitution 2] ❶ a pair of sneakers   ❷ shoes are not comfortable.   ❸ Shoes Are Us
❹ they sell stylish shoes   ❺ having a big sale now   ❻ No problem.

Shopping Unit 11

Practice

Asking for Suggestions

- Any ideas/suggestions?
- Do you have any ideas/suggestions?
- Where do you recommend?
- Which store should I go to?
- Could you give me some advice?

Making Suggestions

- How about ...?
- You can go to ...
- If I were you, I'd ...
- The best place/store would be ...

Responding to Suggestions

[Accepting]
- Sounds good/nice/great.
- I didn't think of that.
- Good/Nice/Great idea! I will give it a try.

[Rejecting]
- Good/Nice/Great idea, but ...

 A Complete the conversation with one of the items below, some expressions from the list above, and your own ideas.

- a comic book
- a hamburger for lunch
- a lunchbox
- a new camera
- a new wallet
- a pair of jeans
- a pair of sneakers
- a pen case
- a suit for job hunting
- a warm winter coat
- fresh vegetables for dinner
- ramen noodles

A: I want to get _____ . _____
　　　　　　　　　 (item)　　　　　　　　　　(ask for a suggestion)

B: _____
　　　(suggest a shopping place)

A: _____
　　　(reject by a bad point)
　　　Any other ideas?

B: Well _____?
　　　　　(suggest a store name)

　　　_____
　　　(tell a good point)

A: _____ . Thanks.
　　　(accept)

B: Anytime.

 B Work in pairs. Read each other's conversation from Task A. Change roles once.

Expanded Conversation

A Think of two people you want to buy presents for. Write their names and favorite things below.

Names	Favorite Things	Partner 1	Partner 2
1.		[Present] [Store]	[Present] [Store]
2.		[Present] [Store]	[Present] [Store]

B Work in pairs. Ask your partner to suggest a present and where to buy it for each person. Write his/her final suggestions in the columns for Partner 1.

Ex
- **A:** I'm thinking about getting a present for my friend Alex. She loves music. Could you give me some advice?
- **B:** If I were you, I'd buy a guitar.
- **A:** Sounds good, but it's too expensive. Any other ideas?
- **B:** Well, how about a music DVD?
- **A:** Great idea! Which store should I go to?
- **B:** If I were you, I'd go to Rock Out. It's close by and convenient.
- **A:** OK. I'll give it a try. Thanks!
- **B:** No problem.

C Change your partner and ask him/her for suggestions. Write their final suggestions in the columns for Partner 2.

D Change you partner again. Discuss the suggestions you received from Partners 1 and 2. Which classmate gave you the best suggestions? Why?

Shopping Unit 11

Short Talk ▸ Opinions about shopping

Listening

A Listen to the short talks by Mariko and Shin. Then answer the questions. 🎧 45–46

	Mariko	Shin
1. Do they like to go shopping?		
2. Where do they like to buy things?		

B Listen again and complete the sentences. 🎧 45–46

1. Mariko's friends help her _____.
2. Shin thinks that big stores are _____.

Speaking

A Prepare for a short talk about your shopping.

- How often do you go shopping?   _____
- How do you feel when you are shopping?   _____
- Who do you go shopping with?   _____
- Do you have favorite stores?   _____
- Do you always buy something, or do you just like to look around?
                                                   _____

B Work in groups. Take turns to give a short talk.

Wrap-up

A How much did you speak in English today? Circle a number.

A little [1]—[2]—[3]—[4]—[5]—[6]—[7] A lot

B Write two words/expressions from this unit that you want to remember.

1. _____   2. _____

85

Unit 12: Strengths and Weaknesses

Asking for help | Talking about abilities

Preparation

A Write the activity matching each picture.

- asking boys/girls on dates
- doing magic tricks
- killing bugs
- saving money
- writing reports
- being on time
- drawing pictures
- making a presentation
- sewing

1. _____

2. _____

3. _____

4. _____

5. _____

6. _____

7. _____

8. _____

9. _____

Strengths and Weaknesses Unit 12

B Are you good at the activities below? Color five stars if you are really great at it, one star if you are hopeless at it.

- cooking ☆☆☆☆☆
- doing homework on time ☆☆☆☆☆
- drawing pictures ☆☆☆☆☆
- playing the piano ☆☆☆☆☆
- singing karaoke ☆☆☆☆☆
- talking to boys/girls ☆☆☆☆☆

- dancing ☆☆☆☆☆
- doing laundry ☆☆☆☆☆
- playing sports ☆☆☆☆☆
- saving money ☆☆☆☆☆
- speaking English ☆☆☆☆☆
- telling jokes ☆☆☆☆☆

C Complete the sentences with some activities from Task B.

1. I'm really good at _____.
2. I'm pretty good at _____.
3. I'm OK at _____.
4. I'm hopeless at _____.

D Work in pairs. Student A, ask your partner the questions below. Student B, answer the questions with your ideas from Task C. Change roles and practice again.

1. What are you really good at?
   I'm really good at …

2. What are you pretty good at?
   I'm pretty good at …

3. What are you OK at?
   I'm OK at …

4. What are you hopeless at?
   I'm hopeless at …

Conversation Model

A Fill in the blanks with the words below. Then listen to the conversation and check your answers.

- good
- help
- hopeless
- think

Hey, Shin. Do you ⓐ_____ you could ❶ kill the bug in the kitchen?

Sure, I'm really ⓑ_____ at ❷ killing bugs.

Good to hear that! Can I ask you any time?

No problem. By the way, could you ⓒ_____ me ❸ stay awake in math class tomorrow?

Sorry, Shin. I'm pretty good at ❹ math but I'm ⓓ_____ at ❺ staying awake in class.

B Work in pairs. Read the conversation with your partner. Change roles once. Then practice again with the substitutions below.

[Substitution 1] ❶ cook dinner ❷ cooking ❸ ask Mariko on a date for me
 ❹ talking to girls ❺ asking girls on dates

[Substitution 2] ❶ go shopping with me ❷ choosing stylish clothes ❸ fix my computer
 ❹ making webpages ❺ fixing computers

Strengths and Weaknesses — Unit 12

Practice

Asking for Help

- **Could you** wash the dishes**?**
- **Would you mind** feeding my goldfish**?**
- **Do you think you could** help me with my math homework**?**
- **Would it be possible for you to** drive me to the station**?**

Responding to Requests

- **Sure,** I can do that for you**.**
- **OK,** I'll give it a try**.**
- **No problem.**
- **I'd love to, but** I have to study for a test**.**
- **Sorry,** I'm hopeless at playing sports**.**
- **No way!** I hate bugs. Do it yourself!

Degree of Strengths and Weaknesses

Strong
1. _____
2. _____
3. _____
4. _____
5. _____
Weak 6. _____

A Complete the list of Degree of Strengths and Weaknesses with these expressions.

- I'm hopeless at math.
- I'm not so good at math.
- I'm OK at math.
- I'm pretty good at math.
- I'm really bad at math.
- I'm really good at math.

B Work in pairs. Practice talking about some activities from Preparation Task B. Use the expressions for strengths and weaknesses above. Try to explain the reasons if there are any.

Ex A: Are you good at <u>telling jokes</u>?
B: No, **I'm really bad at** <u>telling jokes</u>, but **I'm pretty good at** <u>cooking</u>. Are you good at <u>cooking</u>?
A: No, **I'm hopeless at** <u>cooking</u> because <u>my mom always cooks for me</u>.

C Change your partner. This time, practice asking for help and responding to requests. Use some expressions from the list above and Preparation Task B.

Ex A: **Would you mind** <u>feeding my goldfish</u>?
B: **Sure,** I can do that**.**
A: Thank you.

Expanded Conversation

A Work in pairs. Take turns to ask for help with the activities below. Use the expressions from the list of Degree of Strengths and Weaknesses.

- ask someone on a date
- cook dinner
- feed your pet snake
- kill the bug
- babysit for your sister
- do your English homework
- help you not sleep in class
- sew a button on your jacket

Ex **A:** Would you mind feeding my pet snake?
B: Sure, I'm pretty good at looking after pets.
A: I'm glad to hear that.
B: By the way, would it be possible for you to sew a button on my jacket?
A: Sorry, I'm hopeless at sewing.

B Talk to your classmates. Find six people to do the performances below and grade them by coloring stars.

Ex **A:** Do you think you could sing an English song for me?
B: Sorry, I'm hopeless at singing English songs. By the way, could you make a paper plane for me?
A: Sure! I'm really good at making paper planes.

1. Name: _____ ▸ talk like Mickey Mouse   ☆☆☆☆☆
2. Name: _____ ▸ tell a funny joke   ☆☆☆☆☆
3. Name: _____ ▸ dance for 10 seconds   ☆☆☆☆☆
4. Name: _____ ▸ whistle like a bird   ☆☆☆☆☆
5. Name: _____ ▸ sing an English song   ☆☆☆☆☆
6. Name: _____ ▸ make a paper plane   ☆☆☆☆☆

C Work in pairs. Compare your results for Task B. Who colored the most stars?

Ex **A:** Who did you ask to tell a funny joke?
B: I asked Tomoki.
A: How was it?
B: He was hopeless! I colored only one star.

Strengths and Weaknesses Unit 12

Short Talk — Personal skills

Listening

A Listen to the short talks by Dan and Alice. Then circle the correct answers for question 1.

	Dan	Alice
1. What are they really good at?	a. Hiragana b. Kanji c. Making sushi	a. Jiu-jitsu b. Karate c. Portuguese
2. What are they hopeless at?		

B Listen again and answer question 2.

Speaking

A Prepare for a short talk about one of your personal skills.

- What skill are you going to talk about?
- When did you first try it?
- Why do you enjoy it?
- How often do you do it?
- What's difficult about it?
- What advice do you have for a beginner?

B Work in groups. Take turns to give a short talk.

A Complete the sentence about your English skill.

My best English skill is _____ because _____.

B Write two words/expressions from this unit that you want to remember.

1. _____ 2. _____

Review of Units 10–12

Unit 10 Restaurants

  Add today's special to each menu.

The Chinese Restaurant

Fried Rice with Shrimp	$10.00
Sweet & Sour Pork	$12.00
Spring Rolls	$7.00
Today's Special: _____	

The Japanese Restaurant

Tempura Set Meal	$12.50
Sashimi Set Meal	$13.00
Grilled Chicken Skewers	$8.50
Today's Special: _____	

The Italian Restaurant

Pizza Margarita	$9.50
Spaghetti Carbonara	$10.50
Mushroom Risotto	$12.00
Today's Special: _____	

The American Restaurant

New York Burger (Double Cheese)	$8.50
Texas Burger (Bacon & Egg)	$9.00
Hawaiian Burger (Pineapple)	$10.00
Today's Special: _____	

Drinks

Cola	$1.20	Hot/Iced Coffee	$2.50
Green Tea	$3.00	Orange Juice	$3.00

Dessert

Ice Cream	$3.50	Apple Pie	$4.50
Tiramisu	$5.00	Cheesecake	$5.00

B Work in pairs. Choose one restaurant and ask your partner about today's special. Take turns to order your food, a drink, and dessert. When you take the customer's role, complain about some problems. Then change the restaurant and practice again.

Unit 11 Shopping

  Work in pairs. Choose some items you want to buy and take turns to ask your partner to suggest shopping places.

- a bowl of ramen noodles
- a cool T-shirt
- a guitar
- a new backpack
- a new camera
- a new rice cooker
- a pair of chopsticks
- a pair of jeans
- a pair of sneakers
- a pizza
- sushi

Review of Units 10–12

B Change your partner. This time, choose one of the items below. Then talk about the best thing to buy and the best store for it.

- a costume for a Halloween party
- a present for Mother's Day
- a present for your best friend
- an interesting book to read

Unit 12 Strengths and Weaknesses

Work in pairs. Take turns to talk about the strengths and weaknesses of the activities below.

- bowling
- cooking curry
- drawing pictures
- making presentations
- playing the piano
- remembering names
- swimming
- using computers
- waking up early

Are you good at ...?

Well, I'm OK at ...

Combined Language Tasks

A Work in a group of three or four. Imagine you are planning Hawaiian Beach Party for your class. Look at the shopping list below, decide the best stores to buy the items, and take notes.

- decorations _____
- Hawaiian shirts _____
- a Hawaiian music CD _____
- snacks and drinks _____

B Look at the tasks at the party, decide who is the best person for each task, and take notes of their names.

- welcoming the guests _____
- making a speech _____
- playing a song on the Ukulele _____
- being the DJ _____
- cooking food on the barbeque _____
- making a party game _____
- dancing the hula _____
- cleaning up afterwards _____

C The party has started and you can order any food and drinks. Take turns to be the staff member and the customer.

Wrap-up Which units were easier or more difficult for you? Make a mark on the lines.

Unit 10: Restaurants   EASY ———— OK ———— DIFFICULT
Unit 11: Shopping   EASY ———— OK ———— DIFFICULT
Unit 12: Strengths and Weaknesses   EASY ———— OK ———— DIFFICULT

Unit 13 Places

Describing features | Talking about upsides and downsides

Preparation

A Look at the adjectives to describe the features of places. Match each adjective to one with an opposite meaning.

- attractive
- built-up
- clean
- convenient
- inexpensive
- lively
- peaceful
- safe
- traditional/historical

- boring
- crowded
- dangerous
- dirty
- expensive
- inconvenient
- modern
- rural
- unattractive

B Look at the nouns to describe the features of places. Check the boxes if you know the meanings. Look up new words in a dictionary.

- ☐ air pollution
- ☐ amusement park
- ☐ aquarium
- ☐ beach
- ☐ big park
- ☐ botanical garden
- ☐ chain store
- ☐ cinema
- ☐ convenience store
- ☐ department store
- ☐ famous historical site
- ☐ food truck
- ☐ heavy traffic
- ☐ hot spring
- ☐ international restaurant
- ☐ lake
- ☐ luxury hotel
- ☐ mountain
- ☐ museum
- ☐ rice field
- ☐ river
- ☐ shopping mall
- ☐ shrine
- ☐ temple
- ☐ trendy café
- ☐ zoo

C Circle any adjectives and nouns above which you can use to describe your hometown.

Places Unit 13

D Complete the sentences with the names of places.

1. _____ is peaceful and traditional.
2. _____ has a lot of tourists.
3. _____ has a cinema, a shopping mall, and trendy cafés.
4. _____ has heavy traffic and air pollution.
5. _____ is lively but expensive.

E Work in pairs. Student A, ask your partner the questions below. Student B, answer the questions with your ideas from Task D. Change roles and practice again. Have you been to these places?

1. Which place is peaceful and traditional?
   I think …

2. Which place has a lot of tourists?
   I think …

3. Which place has a cinema, a shopping mall, and trendy cafés?
   I think …

4. Which place has heavy traffic and air pollution?
   I think …

5. Which place is lively but expensive?
   I think …

Conversation Model

A Fill in the blanks with the words below. Then listen to the conversation and check your answers.

- best
- downsides
- most
- there are

B Work in pairs. Read the conversation with your partner. Change roles once. Then practice again with the substitutions below.

[Substitution 1] ❶ to France ❷ Paris ❸ interesting and historical
❹ markets ❺ the Eiffel Tower ❻ there are too many tourists

[Substitution 2] ❶ to Japan ❷ Hokkaido ❸ snowy and beautiful
❹ ski resorts ❺ Sapporo Snow Festival ❻ winter is very long

Places Unit 13

Practice

Asking about Places

- **What's** New York **like?**
- **What is the best/worst thing about** Tokyo?
- **What do you like the most?**
- **What are the upsides/downsides?**
- **Is it** attractive?
- **Is there a** museum?
- **Are there any** hot springs?
- **Are there a lot of** chain stores?

Describing Features

- **It's** peaceful **and** safe.
- **It's** exciting **but** dangerous.
- **There is a** shopping mall.
- **There are a few** parks.
- **There is a lot of** heavy traffic.
- **There are a lot of** department stores.
- **There aren't any** cinemas.

Talking about Upsides and Downsides

[Upsides]
- **The best thing about** Paris **is** the Eiffel Tower.
- **One upside is** there are lots of trendy cafés.
- **Another good point is** it's convenient.

[Downsides]
- **The worst thing about** Paris **is** there are too many tourists.
- **One downside is** the heavy traffic.
- **Another bad point is** there is a lot of air pollution.

 Work in pairs. Look at the pictures and information below and practice describing the features of places. Use some words from Preparation Tasks A and B, the expressions from the list above, and your own ideas.

 A: **What's** Paris **like?**
B: **It's** very exciting **and** safe. Also, **there are a lot of** trendy cafés.
A: **What is the best thing about** Paris?
B: **One upside is** there are many historical spots.
A: **What is the worst thing about** Paris?
B: **One downside is** the museums are crowded.

Okinawa, Japan
+ Beautiful beaches
− Lots of chain stores
Famous Site: Kabira Bay

Tokyo, Japan
+ Many reasonable restaurants
− Crowded trains
Famous Site: Sensoji Temple

Kyoto, Japan
+ Lots of historical streets in Gion
− Many tourists
Famous Site: Kiyomizu-dera Temple

B Change your partner and practice again using the pictures and information below.

London, UK
+ Lots of parks and museums
− Expensive restaurants
Famous Site: Big Ben

Rome, Italy
+ Interesting markets
− Heavy traffic
Famous Site: The Colosseum

Agra, India
+ Delicious curry shops
− A lot of air pollution
Famous Site: Taj Mahal

Expanded Conversation

 A Work in pairs. Take turns to describe the last place you visited.

Ex
A: What's the last place you visited like?
B: The last place I visited is Osaka. There are a lot of shops. It's a little crowded.
A: Does it have any famous sites?
B: It has …

B Work in a group of three or four. Student A, think of a famous place in the world. Other students, ask him/her some questions to guess the name of place. After finding out the answer, change roles and practice again.

Ex
A: OK, I'm ready!
B: Is it crowded?
A: Yes, there are many tourists.
C: Are there any beaches?
A: No, there aren't any beaches.
D: Is it modern?
A: Hmm, I think it's more historical.
B: Are there any temples?
A: Yes! There are a lot of temples.
C: Hmm, is it Kyoto?
A: Yes! You got it!

Places | Unit 13

Short Talk ▸ Hometown

Listening

A Listen to the short talks by Dan and Mariko. Then circle the correct answers for questions 1 and 2.

	Dan	Mariko
1. What is one positive?	a. Hiking spots b. Exciting c. Restaurants	a. Great beaches b. Reasonable c. Convenient
2. What is one negative?	a. Expensive b. Earthquakes c. Many tourists	a. Crowded trains b. Dangerous c. Boring
3. What does each place have?	There are a few _____, _____, and quite a few _____.	There are a lot of _____ _____ and a few _____.

B Listen again and complete the answers for question 3.

Speaking

A Prepare for a short talk about your hometown. Use the words you circled in Preparation Tasks A and B.

- Where is your hometown?
- What are some features of your hometown?
- What is the best thing about living there?
- What are the downsides?

B Work in groups. Take turns to give a short talk. Ask your classmates some questions about their hometowns. Ask each other some extra questions too.

Wrap-up

A What English skill do you want to practice more? Why?

B Write two words/expressions from this unit that you want to remember.

1. _____   2. _____

Unit 14 Vacations

Talking about travel plans | Explaining intentions

Preparation

- Barcelona
- ~~Beijing~~
- Honolulu
- Lima
- Nairobi
- New York
- Phnom Penh
- Sydney

A Complete the sentences with the names of places. Then match the names of sightseeing spots to the pictures.

Ex [e] Beijing is the capital of China. It's famous for the Great Wall of China and the **Forbidden City**.

1. [ ] _____ is the biggest city in Australia. **Sydney Opera House** is a popular sightseeing spot.

2. [ ] _____ is the capital of Kenya. Many tourists visit there to go to the **Masai Mara National Reserve**.

3. [ ] Tourists who visit _____ often go to **Broadway** to see musicals.

4. [ ] _____ is the capital of Peru, but most visitors go to the ancient Inca city, **Machu Picchu**, high up in the Andes.

5. [ ] _____ is the capital of Hawaii and famous for **Waikiki Beach**.

6. [ ] **Angkor Wat** is a UNESCO World Heritage Site in Cambodia. It takes about seven hours by bus from the capital _____.

7. [ ] _____ has one of the Spain's most famous soccer teams, and is also famous for the church called **Sagrada Familia**.

a   b   c   d
~~e~~   f   g   h

Vacations Unit 14

B Which activities do you like to do on your vacations? According to your intentions, put ○ (want to), △ (maybe), or ✕ (don't want to) in each box.

- eat at a fancy restaurant ☐
- go shopping ☐
- go to a theme park ☐
- rent a scooter ☐
- visit some museums ☐

- eat street food ☐
- go sightseeing ☐
- go to the beach ☐
- stay in an expensive hotel ☐
- watch live sports ☐

- go camping ☐
- go to a market ☐
- rent a car ☐
- visit nature spots ☐

C Complete the sentences with some words from Tasks A and B.

1. I'd love to visit _____ on vacation someday.
2. I'm definitely going to _____ there.
3. I hope I can _____ there.
4. I don't think I will _____ there.

D Work in pairs. Student A, ask your partner the questions below. Student B, answer the questions with your ideas from Task C. Change roles and practice again.

1. Which place would you like to visit on vacation?
   I'd love to visit ...

2. What do you want to do there?
   I'm definitely going to ...

3. What else would you like to do?
   I hope I can ...

4. What don't you want to do there?
   I don't think I will ...

Conversation Model

A Fill in the blanks with the words below. Then listen to the conversation and check your answers.

- anywhere
- before
- definitely
- planning

Are you going ⓐ_____ this winter?

I'm going to ❶ the Gold Coast in ❷ Australia with June.

Have you been there ⓑ_____?

No. I've always wanted to visit.

What are you ⓒ_____ to do there?

I'm ⓓ_____ going to ❸ go surfing. There are some amazing ❹ surf spots.

You know, ❷ Australia is famous for ❺ dangerous animals.

What else are you going to do?

I hope I can try some local food.

Yeah, I hope I don't ❻ see any sharks.

B Work in pairs. Read the conversation with your partner. Change roles once. Then practice again with the substitutions below.

[Substitution 1] ❶ Chicago ❷ America ❸ visit art galleries
❹ works of art ❺ junk food ❻ get fat

[Substitution 2] ❶ Seoul ❷ Korea ❸ go shopping
❹ bargains ❺ spicy dishes ❻ get a stomach ache

Vacations Unit 14

Practice

Talking about Travel Plans

- **Are you going anywhere** this winter?
- **Where are you going** this winter?
- **Have you ever been there before?**
- **What are you planning to do there?**
- **What else are you going to do?**
- **Where else are you going to go?**
- **Are you going to** do anything else?

- **I'm going to** Australia with June.
- **I'm going to** Spain during New Year holidays.
- **Yes. I've been there** once.   ■ **No. I've never been there.**
- I'm definitely going to go surfing.
- I hope I can try some local food.
- I may go to the Sydney Opera House as well.
- I'm probably going to drink snake wine.

Explaining Intentions

[Want to]
- I'm definitely going to …
- I'm probably going to …

[Maybe]
- I hope I can …
- I may …
- If there's enough time, I want to …

[Don't Want to]
- I hope I don't …
- I don't think I will …
- I'm definitely not going to …

 A Work in pairs. Practice talking about travel plans. Use some expressions from the list above.

Ex
A: **Where are you going** this winter?
B: I'm going to …
A: Have you been there before?
B: Yes/No. …
A: What are you planning to do there?
B: I'm probably going to …
A: What else are you going to do?
B: I may …
A: Where else are you going to go?
B: If there's enough time, I want to go to …
A: **Are you going to** eat …?
B: I don't think I will eat …

 B Choose one of the places below. According to your intentions, put ○, △, or ✕ for each activity. Then take turns to ask about your partner's travel plans.

Beijing
- visit the Great Wall
- eat Peking duck
- rent a bicycle
- see the Forbidden City
- drink Chinese wine
- stay in an expensive hotel

Honolulu
- go scuba diving
- take hula dancing classes
- eat fresh seafood
- buy a Hawaiian shirt
- go fishing
- rent a car

C Change your partner. Choose one of the places below and practice again.

Sydney
- take English lessons
- go surfing
- have a beach barbeque
- visit national park
- watch rugby
- see a big spider

Phnom Penh
- visit Angkor Wat
- do volunteer work
- go to a night market
- rent a scooter
- drink snake wine
- eat street food

Expanded Conversation

 A Make travel plans for your vacations. Write some activities according to your intentions.

Ex Summer Vacation	Winter Vacation	Spring Vacation
[Plan] London (2 weeks)	[Plan]	[Plan]
[Want to] – visit Big Ben – eat fish and chips	[Want to]	[Want to]
[Maybe] – take a boat ride on the Thames – have afternoon tea	[Maybe]	[Maybe]
[Don't Want to] – rent a car – watch soccer games	[Don't Want to]	[Don't Want to]

B Work in pairs. Take turns to talk about your travel plans.

Vacations Unit 14

Short Talk ▸ Vacation plans

Listening

A Listen to the short talks by Shin and Alice. Then answer questions 1 and 2. 🎧 57–58

	Shin	Alice
1. Where are they going during their vacations?		
2. How long will they stay?		
3. What will they do?	a. Eat meat b. Go hiking c. Go skiing d. Stay at his grandmother's house	a. Eat junk food b. See a musical c. See the Statue of Liberty d. Watch a baseball match

B Listen again and circle the correct answers for question 3. There may be more than one answer. 🎧 57–58

Speaking

A Imagine you are going to a place you have always wanted to visit. Prepare for a short talk about your vacation plan.

- Where and when are you going? _____
- Who would you like to go with? _____
- Where will you stay? _____
- What would you like to do? _____
- Is there anything you don't want to do? _____

B Work in groups. Take turns to give a short talk.

Wrap-up

A Complete the sentence by circling one of the expressions.

[I'm definitely going to / I may / I don't think I will] speak English fluently in the future.

B Write two words/expressions from this unit that you want to remember.

1. _____ 2. _____

105

Unit 15 Experiences

Talking about past events | Describing feelings

Preparation

A Look at each set of adjectives to describe feelings. Check the boxes if you know the meanings. Look up new words in a dictionary.

- ☐ amazed / amazing
- ☐ bored / boring
- ☐ excited / exciting
- ☐ interested / interesting
- ☐ scared / scary
- ☐ surprised / surprising
- ☐ annoyed / annoying
- ☐ disappointed / disappointing
- ☐ impressed / impressive
- ☐ satisfied / satisfying
- ☐ shocked / shocking
- ☐ tired / tiring

B Read the information below and complete each sentence by circling one of the adjectives.

> The adjectives you use to describe feelings about experiences are different depending on the subject.
>
> **[People]** I was **amazed**. / We were **scared**.
> **[Things]** Scuba diving was **amazing**. / The movies were **scary**.

1. I watched a great movie yesterday. It was really [interested / interesting].
2. We just saw a snake. We were really [scared / scary].
3. My friend made a presentation last week. It was really [impressed / impressive].
4. I read a few books but all of them were [bored / boring].
5. I was kind of [tired / tiring] when I woke up this morning. Studying every day is really [tired / tiring].
6. My wallet was stolen by someone. It was so [shocked / shocking].

Experiences Unit 15

C Imagine you went somewhere with someone during the last vacation. Write the name of the place below and complete sentences 1–5.

[Place] _____

1. [Partner]   I went with _____.
2. [Transportation] We went there by _____.
3. [Event]   We _____.
4. [Scenery]   We saw _____.
5. [Food]   We ate _____.

D Work in pairs. Student A, ask your partner questions 1–5 and guess where he/she went. Student B, answer the questions with your ideas from Task C. Change roles and practice again.

1. Who did you go with?
   I went with …

2. How did you get there?
   We went there by …

3. What did you do?
   We …

4. What did you see?
   We saw …

5. What did you eat?
   We ate …

6. OK, I think you went to …
   Yes, I did. / No, I didn't. Guess again!

Conversation Model

A Fill in the blanks with the words below. Then listen to the conversation and check your answers.

- did you
- flight
- go with
- trip

Hi, June. How was your ⓐ_____ to Australia?

It was so fun.

How was your ⓑ_____?

Well, ❶ it took 10 hours, so I was really ❷ tired.

That's too bad. Who did you ⓒ_____?

I went with Mariko. We stayed ❸ in a small hotel.

So, ⓓ_____ try scuba diving?

Yeah. We saw ❹ a lot of fish. It was really ❺ amazing.

Wow!

B Work in pairs. Read the conversation with your partner. Change roles once. Then practice again with the substitutions below.

[Substitution 1] ❶ the person behind me was too loud ❷ annoyed
                  ❸ at a campground ❹ a huge turtle ❺ surprising

[Substitution 2] ❶ the movies were not interesting ❷ bored
                  ❸ in a resort ❹ a big shark ❺ scary

Experiences Unit 15

Practice

🎧 60

Asking about Past Events

- **How was your trip to** your hometown?
- **How did you get there?**
- **Who did you go with?**
- **What did you do** in Australia?
- **Did you** go hiking?
- **Did you have a good time** in Australia?
- **How was the** food/flight/hotel/sea/weather?
- **Where did you stay?**
- **Did you enjoy** scuba diving?

Describing Feelings

[Positive]
1. amazed / _____
2. excited / _____
3. _____ / impressive
4. interested / interesting
5. _____ / _____
6. surprised / _____

[Negative]
1. _____ / annoying
2. _____ / boring
3. disappointed / disappointing
4. _____ / _____
5. shocked / _____
6. _____ / tiring

A Complete the list for Describing Feelings with the adjectives from Preparation Task A.

B Work in pairs. Imagine you went to one of the places below. Take turns to ask questions and describe feelings. Use the questions and adjectives from the list above.

Ex A: **How was your trip to** Kenya?
    B: It was so <u>exciting</u>.
    A: **Who did you go with?**
    B: I went with my family.
    A: **Where did you stay?**
    B: We stayed in a nice hotel in the city.
    A: **What did you do** there?
    B: We went to the Masai Mara National Reserve and saw a lot of wild animals. They were really <u>amazing</u>.
    A: Wow!

Barcelona   Beijing

New York   Sydney

C Change your partner. This time, practice describing feelings about several events in your trip. Student A, look at page 111. Student B, look at page 112.

Expanded Conversation

A Talk to three classmates. Ask them the questions below and make notes of their answers. Use information from Preparation Task C when you answer.

Questions	Classmate 1	Classmate 2	Classmate 3
1. Where did you go?			
2. Who did you go with?			
3. How did you get there? How was it?			
4. What did you see? How was it?			
5. What did you do? How was it?			
6. What did you eat? How was it?			
7. Overall, how was the experience?			

B Which classmate had the most fun experience? Why? Discuss with another partner.

Experiences Unit 15

Student A

You traveled to Paris. Look at each event below and decide if it was good or not. Then write the reasons with the adjectives to describe feelings.

Events	Feelings	Reasons
1. You flew to Paris.	☺ ☹	
2. You stayed in an expensive hotel.	☺ ☹	
3. You climbed to the top of the Eiffel Tower.	☺ ☹	
4. You saw the Mona Lisa in the Louvre.	☺ ☹	
5. You ate French food.	☺ ☹	

II Now, answer your partner's questions about your trip to Paris.

III Your partner traveled to Vancouver. Ask him/her the questions and write his/her feelings.

Questions	Your Partner's Feelings
1. How was your flight?	
2. Where did you stay? How was it?	
3. What did you do in Vancouver? How was it?	
4. Did you go snowboarding? How was it?	
5. What did you eat? How was it?	

Student B

 You traveled to Vancouver. Look at each event below and decide if it was good or not. Then write the reasons with the adjectives to describe feelings.

Events	Feelings	Reasons
1. You flew to Vancouver.	☺ ☹	
2. You stayed with a Canadian family.	☺ ☹	
3. You took some English lessons.	☺ ☹	
4. You went snowboarding and saw a bear.	☺ ☹	
5. You ate maple syrup cookies.	☺ ☹	

II **Your partner traveled to Paris. Ask him/her the questions and write his/her feelings.**

Questions	Your Partner's Feelings
1. How was your flight?	
2. Where did you stay? How was it?	
3. What did you do in Paris? How was it?	
4. Did you go to a museum? How was it?	
5. What did you eat? How was it?	

 Now, answer your partner's questions about your trip to Vancouver.

Experiences Unit 15

Short Talk ▸ Memories from a trip

Listening

A Listen to the short talks by Mariko and Mark. Then answer the questions. 🎧 61-62

	Mariko	Mark
1. Where did they go?		
2. Who did they travel with?		
3. How long did they stay?		

B Listen again and complete the sentences. 🎧 61-62

1. Mariko stayed at a hotel and it was very _____ for sightseeing. She was really surprised to see a lot of _____ from all over the world.

2. Mark's travel by train was _____ but the food tasted _____.

Speaking

A Prepare for a short talk about the memories from your trip.

- Where did you go? _____
- Who did you go with? _____
- Where did you stay? _____
- What did you do? _____
- Was it a good experience? Why or why not? _____

B Work in groups. Take turns to give a short talk.

Wrap-up

A Complete the sentence with some adjectives from Preparation Task A.

This unit was _____ and _____.

B Write two words/expressions from this unit that you want to remember.

1. _____ 2. _____

Review of Units 13–15

Unit 13 Places

A Write the adjectives with opposite meanings to describe the features of places. Then look at Preparation Task A on page 94 to check your answers.

- attractive ↔ _____
- built-up ↔ _____
- convenient ↔ _____
- expensive ↔ _____
- traditional/historical ↔ _____

- boring ↔ _____
- clean ↔ _____
- crowded ↔ _____
- safe ↔ _____

B Work in pairs. Take turns to ask about your partner's favorite place and make some notes below.

What's ... like?   Is there a ...?   Are there any ...?   What are the upsides/downsides?

[Name]   My partner's favorite place is _____.
[Features]   It's _____ and _____.
             There is a _____.
             There are _____.
             There aren't any _____.
[Upsides]   One upside is _____.
[Downsides] One downside is _____.

Unit 14 Vacations

A Look at the expressions to explain intentions and put ○ (want to), △ (maybe), or ✕ (don't want to). Then look at the list on page 103 to check your answers.

- I don't think I will ... ☐
- I hope I don't ... ☐
- If there's enough time, I want to ... ☐
- I'm definitely not going to ... ☐

- I hope I can ... ☐
- I may ... ☐
- I'm definitely going to ... ☐
- I'm probably going to ... ☐

B Work in pairs. Imagine you are going to visit your partner's favorite place. Look at your notes above and take turns to talk about your travel plans.

Review of Units 13–15

Unit 15 | Experiences

Work in pairs. Imagine you visited your favorite place. Take turns to ask questions and describe feelings about your trip.

Where did you go?
Who did you go with?
How did you get there?
Where did you stay?
What did you do?
How was it?

Combined Language Tasks

A Imagine you won a lottery and are going on a world trip. Circle three destinations and draw a line from your departure point.

B Write some activities according to your intentions. Then work in pairs. Take turns to talk about your travel plans. Remember you are very rich.

Destination 1	Destination 2	Destination 3
○	○	○
△	△	△
✕	✕	✕

C Change your partners. Imagine you came back from the world trip. Take turns to talk about your experiences.

Wrap-up

Which units were easier or more difficult for you? Make a mark on the lines.

Unit 13: Places   EASY —— OK —— DIFFICULT
Unit 14: Vacations   EASY —— OK —— DIFFICULT
Unit 15: Experiences   EASY —— OK —— DIFFICULT

Unit 16 Opinions

Making comparisons | Agreeing and disagreeing

Preparation

A Read the information below and write comparative adjectives in the columns.

[Comparative Adjectives]

You can use comparative adjectives to compare two things. There are three ways to change adjectives to the comparative form.

1. Add "er" after the adjective with one syllable.
   - fast ▶ fast**er**   - small ▶ small**er**

2. Change "y" to "ier" at the end of adjectives ending with "y."
   - bus**y** ▶ bus**ier**   - tast**y** ▶ tast**ier**

3. Add "more/less" before the adjective with more than one syllable.
   - convenient ▶ **more/less** convenient   - expensive ▶ **more/less** expensive

[Syllables]

Every English word has one or more syllables. An easy way to count the number is to place your hand under your chin when you say the word. How many times does your chin touch your hand? That is the number of syllables. Try it with the words below.

- fast —— (1)   - tir | ing —— (2)   - con | ve | nient —— (3)

■ beautiful	■ boring	■ busy	■ ~~cheap~~	■ costly	■ crowded
■ cute	■ delicious	■ exciting	■ friendly	■ funny	■ healthy
■ important	■ inconvenient	■ lively	■ loud	■ memorable	■ weird

-er	-ier	more/less
cheaper		

Opinions Unit 16

B Complete the sentences with your own ideas.

1. [The Best Place for a Short Trip]

   It seems to me that _____
   _____.

2. [A Good Topic for Writing a Report]

   If you ask me, _____
   _____.

3. [A Good Souvenir from Japan]

   The way I see it, _____
   _____.

4. [The Best Place to Live]

   In my opinion, _____
   _____.

C Work in pairs. Student A, ask your partner the questions below. Student B, answer the questions with your ideas from Task B. Change roles and practice again.

1. Where is the best place for a short trip?

   It seems to me that …

2. What is a good topic for writing a report?

   If you ask me, …

3. What is a good souvenir from Japan?

   The way I see it, …

4. Where is the best place to live?

   In my opinion, …

Conversation Model

A Fill in the blanks with the words below. Then listen to the conversation and check your answers.

- ask
- difficult
- true
- which

Hey, Mark, ⓐ_____ ❶ place for a trip do you think is better, ❷ Disneyland or ❸ a hot spring?

❷ Disneyland or ❸ a hot spring? That's a ⓑ_____ question. If you ⓒ_____ me, ❷ Disneyland is better because it's ❹ more exciting.

Really? It's so ❺ crowded.

That's ⓓ_____, but ❻ I like it anyway.

Well, I don't really agree with you.

B Work in pairs. Read the conversation with your partner. Change roles once. Then practice again with the substitutions below.

[Substitution 1] ❶ souvenir for my dad   ❷ an Aloha shirt   ❸ coffee beans
                  ❹ memorable   ❺ loud   ❻ I think Aloha shirts look really cool

[Substitution 2] ❶ place to live   ❷ the city   ❸ the country
                  ❹ more convenient   ❺ costly   ❻ the countryside is less exciting

Practice

Asking about Opinions

- **Which** sport **do you think is better,** baseball **or** basketball**?**
- **What's your opinion on** video games**?**
- **What do you think about** living in the country**?**
- **Do you agree with me?**

Agreeing and Disagreeing

Agree
- Definitely.
- That's a good point.
- I think so too.
- That's true, but ...
- Well maybe, but ...
- I don't really agree with you.

Disagree
- No way!

Expressing Opinions

- **It seems to me that** ...
- **If you ask me,** ...
- **The way I see it,** ...
- **In my opinion,** ...

A Look at each topic and a set of choices. Then circle the better choice for you and write the reason with a comparative adjective from Preparation Task A.

1. [Sport]   [baseball / basketball]

2. [Pet]   [dogs / cats]

3. [Dish]   [udon / ramen]

4. [Season]   [spring / fall]

5. [Pastime]   [watching movies / playing video games]

B Work in pairs. Practice talking about comparisons. Use the topics from Task A and the expressions from the list above.

Ex
A: **Which** sport **do you think is better,** baseball **or** basketball**?**
B: **If you ask me,** basketball **is better** because it's <u>more exciting</u>.
A: I think so too. / No way!

C Change your partner. This time, use the topics from Preparation Task B. Tell your partner the reasons why you agree or disagree with his/her opinions.

Expanded Conversation

A Work in pairs. Your teacher will give you a dice (or six cards). Student A, imagine one of the statements below is your opinion and read it out. Student B, agree or disagree according to the number on the dice. Try to add a reason too. Change roles and practice again.

1. Studying English is more important than studying math.
2. Japanese people are shy.
3. Doria is the most delicious Japanese food.
4. Everyone should get married.
5. Japanese food is healthy.
6. Reading books is less interesting than watching TV.
7. University is boring.
8. Cooking at home is better than eating out.

⚀	Definitely.	⚁	That's a good point.
⚂	I think so too.	⚄	That's true, but …
⚄	I don't really agree with you.	⚅	No way!

B Change your partner. Complete the statements with your own ideas. Then take turns to discuss each topic. Give the reasons why you agree or disagree.

1. _____ is more important than _____.
2. _____ people are _____.
3. _____ is the most delicious _____ food.
4. Everyone should _____.
5. Japanese food is _____.
6. _____ is less interesting than _____.
7. University is _____.
8. _____ is better than _____.

Opinions Unit 16

Short Talk ▸ The best way to relax

Listening

A Listen to the short talks by Shin and Yolanda. Then answer the question.

	Shin	Yolanda
Where do they like to go to relax?		

B Listen again and confirm if the statements are true or false.

1. There are no hot springs in Shin's hometown. [T / F]
2. Shin usually spends a short time at a hot spring. [T / F]
3. Yolanda likes sandy beaches. [T / F]
4. Yolanda thinks Hawaiian coffee is delicious. [T / F]

Speaking

A Prepare for a short talk about the best way to relax.

What is the best way for you to relax?
_____

Why do you think so? Write a few reasons.
_____
_____

B Work in groups. Take turns to give a short talk.

A Complete the sentence with your own ideas.

In my opinion, this unit was _____.

B Write two words/expressions from this unit that you want to remember.

1. _____ 2. _____

Unit 17

Health and Illness

Talking about health problems › Giving advice

Preparation

A Write the symptom matching each picture.

- coughing
- feverish
- headache
- itchy eyes
- nauseous
- runny nose
- sneezing
- sore throat
- stomach ache

1. _____

2. _____

3. _____

4. _____

5. _____

6. _____

7. _____

8. _____

9. _____

Health and Illness Unit 17

B Complete the sentences with your own ideas.

1. [Frequency]   I get sick _____.
2. [Symptoms]   I usually have _____ when I catch a cold.
3. [Things to Do]   I _____ when I catch a cold.
4. [Good Habit]   My good health habit is _____.
5. [Bad Habit]   My bad health habit is _____.

C Work in pairs. Student A, ask your partner the questions below. Student B, answer the questions with your ideas from Task B. Change roles and practice again.

1. How often do you get sick?

   I get sick …

2. What symptoms do you have when you catch a cold?

   I usually have … when I catch a cold.

3. What do you do when you catch a cold?

   I … when I catch a cold.

4. What is one of your good health habits?

   My good health habit is …

5. What is one of your bad health habits?

   My bad health habit is …

Conversation Model

A Fill in the blanks with the words below. Then listen to the conversation and check your answers.

- alright
- feverish
- medicine
- sore throat

Alice! ❶ What's up?

Hi, Mark. I'm not feeling well today. I have a ⓐ_____ and ❷ a runny nose.

Are you ⓑ_____? Maybe you caught a cold.

Yeah. I was feeling fine yesterday, but this morning I felt ⓒ_____ and ❸ had a headache.

You should go home and rest. Do you have any ⓓ_____?

❹ Maybe not.

Come on. I'll drive you home. ❺ Let's stop by the drugstore.

B Work in pairs. Read the conversation with your partner. Change roles once. Then practice again with the substitutions below.

[Substitution 1] ❶ What's wrong? ❷ I can't stop sneezing ❸ had a stomachache
❹ I don't remember. ❺ Maybe you ought to see a doctor.

[Substitution 2] ❶ You don't look very well. ❷ I can't stop coughing ❸ felt nauseous
❹ Yeah, I have some. ❺ You'd better take it easy today.

Health and Illness Unit 17

Practice

Asking about Physical Condition	Talking about Health Problems
▪ **How are you feeling** today? ▪ You **don't look very well**. What's up? ▪ **What's wrong?** ▪ **Are you alright?** ▪ **Do you have** hay fever? ▪ **Are you feeling** nauseous? ▪ **Are you** sneezing?	▪ **I have a** sore throat. ▪ **I have** itchy eyes. ▪ **I feel** feverish. ▪ **I can't stop** sneezing. ▪ My neck is **itchy**. ▪ My leg **hurts**.
Giving Advice	Talking about Health Habits
▪ **You should** go home and rest. ▪ **You ought to** see a doctor. ▪ **You'd better** drink lots of water. ▪ **You need to** take some medicine. ▪ **You shouldn't** do any sports. ▪ **Don't** eat oily food. ▪ **Avoid** junk food.	▪ **I always** take a bath in the evening. ▪ **I always** gargle **when I** get home. ▪ **I exercise at least** twice a week. ▪ **I try to avoid** junk food. ▪ **I almost never** drink coffee.

A Work in pairs. Look at one of the pictures in Preparation Task A. Take turns to act out the symptom and guess what your partner is acting.

B Practice talking about health problems and giving advice. Use the symptoms from Preparation Task A and the expressions from the list above.

> **Ex** A: **How are you feeling today?**
> B: I'm not feeling well. I think **I have** ...
> A: **What's wrong?**
> B: ... (talk about symptoms)
> A: **Do you have** ...?
> B: Yes, I do. / No, I don't.
> A: ... (give advice)

C Change your partner. This time, practice talking about health problems and guessing the illness. Student A, look at page 127. Student B, look at page 128.

> **Ex** A: **You don't look very well. What's up?**
> B: ... (talk about three symptoms)
> A: ... (ask about another symptom)
> B: Yes/No, I ...
> A: Well, I think **you have** heatstroke. ... (give advice)

Expanded Conversation

A Work in class. Take turns to ask your teacher the survey questions and make notes of his/her answers. Then give him/her a health rating. Color five stars if he/she is really healthy, one star if he/she is unhealthy.

B Write your own answers below. Then give yourself a health rating.

Survey Questions	Teacher	You	Partner 1	Partner 2
1. How often do you get sick?				
2. Do you eat fruit and vegetables every day?				
3. Do you eat a lot of junk food and snacks?				
4. What is your favorite junk food?				
5. How many hours do you usually sleep?				
6. When do you exercise?				
7. What kind of exercise do you do?				
8. What's the most important thing for good health?				
Health Rating	☆☆☆☆☆	☆☆☆☆☆	☆☆☆☆☆	☆☆☆☆☆

C Work in pairs. Ask your partner the survey questions and make notes of his/her answers in the columns for Partner 1. Then give him/her a health rating and exchange health advice with each other.

D Change your partner and practice again. Use the columns for Partner 2. Does he/she give you the same advice as Partner 1?

Health and Illness Unit 17

Student A

I Your partner doesn't look well today. Ask about his/her physical condition, guess the illness from the list, and give advice.

- a cold
- food poisoning
- hay fever
- heatstroke

II You are not feeling well today. Look at the pictures and tell your partner about your symptoms.

III Your partner doesn't look well today. Ask about his/her physical condition, guess the illness from the list, and give advice.

- a cold
- food poisoning
- hay fever
- heatstroke

IV You are not feeling well today. Look at the pictures and tell your partner about your symptoms.

Student B

I You are not feeling well today. Look at the pictures and tell your partner about your symptoms.

II Your partner doesn't look well today. Ask about his/her physical condition, guess the illness from the list, and give advice.

- a cold
- food poisoning
- hay fever
- heatstroke

III You are not feeling well today. Look at the pictures and tell your partner about your symptoms.

IV Your partner doesn't look well today. Ask about his/her physical condition, guess his/her illness from the list, and give advice.

- a cold
- food poisoning
- hay fever
- heatstroke

Health and Illness Unit 17

Short Talk ▸ Good health habits

Listening

A Listen to the short talks by Shin and June. Then circle the correct answers for question 1.

	Shin	June
1. Which statement is true?	a. He exercises regularly. b. He loves junk food. c. He often gets sick.	a. She cooks hot soup. b. She drinks cold drinks. c. She never gets sick.
2. What is the most important thing for them to stay healthy?		

B Listen again and answer question 2.

Speaking

A Prepare for a short talk about your good health habits.

- I think it is good to _____.
- I think _____ is very important.
- I always _____ in the morning/evening.
- I _____ _____ times a week.
- I always _____ when I _____.
- I try to avoid _____.
- I almost never _____.

B Work in groups. Take turns to give a short talk.

Wrap-up

A If you get sick, do you think you can explain your symptoms to a doctor in English?

YES ———— MAYBE ———— NO

B Write two words/expressions from this unit that you want to remember.

1. _____ 2. _____

Unit 18 The Future

Talking about dreams and goals ⟩ Making time references

Preparation

A Write the name of job matching each picture.

- athlete
- care worker
- computer specialist
- designer
- doctor
- fire fighter
- flight attendant
- househusband
- lawyer
- movie director
- office worker
- personal trainer

1. _____

2. _____

3. _____

4. _____

5. _____

6. _____

7. _____

8. _____

9. _____

10. _____

11. _____

12. _____

The Future Unit 18

B **Complete Shin's future plans with the time references below.**

- after I graduate
- five years from now
- in my 30's

Next year, _____, I'm planning to go back to Japan and find a job as a tour guide. I want to get lots of experience there and I'd like to come back to Hawaii _____. Then I'd like to start my own company when I'm _____.

C **Think of one cool job and one boring job. Then write each job and the reason why you think it is cool or boring.**

[Cool Job] _____

_____

[Boring Job] _____

_____

D **Work in pairs. Student A, ask your partner the questions below. Student B, answer the questions with your ideas from Task C. Change roles and practice again.**

1. What do you think is a cool job?
   I think ... is a cool job.

2. Why do you think so?
   Because ...

3. What do you think is a boring job?
   I think ... is a boring job.

4. Why do you think so?
   Because ...

Conversation Model

A Fill in the blanks with the words below. Then listen to the conversation and check your answers.

- actually
- getting
- hope
- planning

Hey, Dan. What do you want to do ❶after graduation?

Well, I'm ⓐ_____ to ❷go snowboarding in Hokkaido. Then, I ⓑ_____ to ❸work as an English teacher in Tokyo.

Sounds great!

Where do you see yourself ❹in 10 years?

I ⓒ_____ want to ❺be a comic artist, so I'm not planning on ⓓ_____ married or having kids yet.

Wow! You are so ❻ambitious!

B Work in pairs. Read the conversation with your partner. Change roles once. Then practice again with the substitutions below.

[Substitution 1]   ❶ in the future   ❷ move to LA   ❸ become an actor
                   ❹ five years from now   ❺ travel around the world   ❻ adventurous

[Substitution 2]   ❶ next year   ❷ do some volunteer work
                   ❸ work for a famous company in the future   ❹ this time next year
                   ❺ become a singer in a band   ❻ cool

The Future Unit 18

Practice

Asking about Dreams and Goals	
▪ **What do you want to do/be** in the future?	▪ **Where do you see yourself** in 10 years?
▪ **Where do you think you'll be** five years from now?	▪ **Would you like to be** a lawyer?

Time References		
▪ **in** the future	▪ **in my/your 20's/30's/40's**	▪ **in** three years
▪ **after** graduation/retirement	▪ **by the year** 2020	▪ five years **from now**

Talking about Dreams and Goals	
[Positive]	[Negative]
▪ **I'm planning to** start a band.	▪ **I don't think I will** work in an office.
▪ **I hope to be** a doctor.	▪ **I'm not planning on** getting married.
▪ **I want to** find true love.	▪ **I wouldn't like to** live somewhere cold.
▪ **I've always wanted to** have a big family.	▪ **I would never want to** live in a foreign country.

 Work in pairs. Practice talking about the future jobs. Use some names of jobs below and expressions from the list above.

▪ athlete	▪ care worker	▪ comedian	▪ computer specialist
▪ designer	▪ doctor	▪ fire fighter	▪ flight attendant
▪ househusband/housewife		▪ lawyer	▪ movie director
▪ newscaster	▪ office worker	▪ personal trainer	▪ teacher ▪ translator

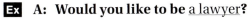

A: **Would you like to be** a lawyer?
B: Yes, **I've always wanted to be** a lawyer because I could make a lot of money.
   Would you like to be a doctor in the future?
A: No, **I wouldn't like to be** a doctor. It's too stressful.

 Change your partner. This time, practice talking about dreams and goals. Student A, look at the information below. Students B, look at the information on page 134.

Student A

	Time References	Dreams and Goals
1	after graduation	planning to travel around Europe
2	three years from now	want to be a flight attendant
3	in 10 years	hope to get married
4	in your 40's	would love to live overseas
5	after retirement	hope to buy an expensive sports car

Student B

	Time References	Dreams and Goals
1	after graduation	planning to study overseas
2	three years from now	want to be a TV newscaster
3	in 10 years	hope to have three kids
4	in your 40's	would love to be a househusband/housewife
5	after retirement	hope to win the Nobel Prize

Expanded Conversation

A Write dreams and goals with your own ideas.

1. [after graduation] _____

2. [three years from now] _____

3. [in 10 years] _____

4. [in your 40's] _____

5. [after retirement] _____

B Work in pairs. Take turns to ask about the dreams and goals from Task A. Try to explain the reasons when you answer.

C Change your partner. This time, take turns to ask about the dreams and goals below. Give reasons and use time references when you can.

- be rich
- stay single
- live in a big city
- live overseas
- start your own business
- write a book

Ex A: Would you like to live overseas?
B: No, I wouldn't like to live overseas. I want to stay near my family. How about you?
A: I'm planning to live overseas three years from now. It's my dream to live in Italy.

The Future Unit 18

Short Talk ▸ Future plans

Listening

A Listen to the short talks by Yolanda and Mariko. Check if the statements are true or false. 🎧 73-74

Yolanda	1. She wants to move back to California in three years.	[T / F]
	2. She wants to be closer to her family.	[T / F]
Mariko	1. She will graduate next year.	[T / F]
	2. She will stop surfing when she gets a job.	[T / F]

B Listen again and complete the sentences. 🎧 73-74

1. Yolanda wants to travel to _____ after she retires.
2. Mariko hopes to be a _____ in Hawaii.

Speaking

A Prepare for a short talk about your future plans.

Write three things you want to do in the future with time references.

1. _____
2. _____
3. _____

B Work in groups. Take turns to give a short talk.

Wrap-up

A Are you going to use English in the future? Why or why not?
_____

B Write two words/expressions from this unit that you want to remember.

1. _____ 2. _____

135

Review of Units 16–18

Unit 16 — Opinions

A Complete the list for Agreeing and Disagreeing with these expressions. Then look at page 119 to check your answers.

- Definitely.
- That's a good point.
- I don't really agree with you.
- That's true, but …
- I think so too.
- Well maybe, but …
- No way!

Agree
1. _____
2. _____
3. _____
4. _____
5. _____
6. _____
Disagree
7. _____

B Work in pairs. Complete the statements with your own ideas. Then take turns to discuss each topic. Give the reasons why you agree or disagree.

1. _____ is the most delicious _____ food.
2. University students should definitely _____.
3. _____ is the most important thing in the world.
4. _____ is better than _____.

Unit 17 — Health and Illness

A Match the first/last halves of the sentences to complete the expressions for health problems. Then look at the list on page 125 to check your answers.

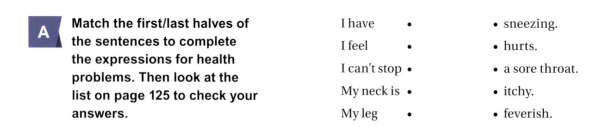

I have	•	• sneezing.
I feel	•	• hurts.
I can't stop	•	• a sore throat.
My neck is	•	• itchy.
My leg	•	• feverish.

B Work in pairs. Imagine you are not feeling well today. Take turns to describe your symptoms and give advice.

Review of Units 16–18

Unit 18 — The Future

A Write your dreams and goals for the future.

1. [before graduation] _____
2. [one year from now] _____
3. [in five years] _____
4. [in your 30's] _____
5. [someday] _____

B Work in pairs. Take turns to ask about the dreams and goals from Task A. Try to explain the reasons when you answer.

Combined Language Tasks

A Complete the statements about health habits and the future with your own opinions.

[Health Habits]
1. Eating _____ every day is healthy.
2. _____ is the best exercise.
3. _____ is bad for your health.

[The Future]
1. _____ is an interesting job.
2. _____ is a boring job.
3. Everyone should try _____ once in their life.

B Work in pairs. Your teacher will give you a dice (or six cards). Take turns to read out one of the statements from Task A. Agree or disagree according to the number on the dice when you respond. Try to add the reasons too.

- ⚀ Definitely.
- ⚄ I think so too.
- ⚅ I don't really agree with you.
- ⚁ That's a good point.
- ⚃ That's true, but …
- ⚂ No way!

Wrap-up Which units were easier or more difficult for you? Make a mark on the lines.

Unit 16: Opinions   EASY———OK———DIFFICULT
Unit 17: Health and Illness EASY———OK———DIFFICULT
Unit 18: The Future   EASY———OK———DIFFICULT

Vocabulary List

A

- [ ] a bit　少し、ちょっと
- [ ] a lot　とても、よく、たくさん
- [ ] ability　能力、才能
- [ ] academic advisor　学習アドバイザー
- [ ] accept　受け入れる、引き受ける
- [ ] across from ...　…の向かいに、…の前に
- [ ] active　行動的な、アクティブな
- [ ] actor　俳優
- [ ] actually　実は
- [ ] adventurous　冒険心のある
- [ ] agree　同意する
- [ ] air pollution　大気汚染
- [ ] always　いつも
- [ ] amaze　びっくりさせる、感心させる
- [ ] amazing　すばらしい
- [ ] ambitious　野心的な
- [ ] amusement park　遊園地
- [ ] ancient　古代の
- [ ] annoy　イライラさせる、困らせる
- [ ] anyway　とりあえず、とにかく
- [ ] appearance　外見、容姿、外観
- [ ] aquarium　水族館
- [ ] arena　競技場
- [ ] arrange a schedule　予定を立てる、計画する
- [ ] art and design　美術・デザイン学
- [ ] art gallery　画廊、美術館
- [ ] artistic　芸術科肌の、美的センスがある
- [ ] athlete　スポーツ選手
- [ ] attractive　魅力的な、感じがいい
- [ ] average　平均的な
- [ ] avoid　避ける
- [ ] awesome　すばらしい

B

- [ ] babysit　子守をする、面倒を見る
- [ ] bald　禿げた
- [ ] bargain　安売り、格安品
- [ ] beach　浜、海辺、海岸
- [ ] beard　あごひげ
- [ ] before　以前に
- [ ] best friend　親友
- [ ] between A and B　AとBの間
- [ ] blonde　金髪
- [ ] bookstore　本屋
- [ ] boring　つまらない
- [ ] borrow　借りる
- [ ] botanical garden　植物園
- [ ] bowl　鉢、椀、どんぶり、ボウル
- [ ] bug　虫
- [ ] build　体格
- [ ] built-up　建物が立ち並んだ
- [ ] burned　焦げた
- [ ] by the way　ところで

C

- [ ] cafeteria　学食、カフェテリア
- [ ] capital　首都
- [ ] care worker　介護職員
- [ ] chain store　チェーン店
- [ ] chat　おしゃべりする
- [ ] cheap　安っぽい、安い
- [ ] choice　品ぞろえ、選択肢
- [ ] choose　選ぶ
- [ ] church　教会
- [ ] cinema　映画館
- [ ] clean-shaven　ひげを剃った
- [ ] climb　登る
- [ ] close by　すぐ近くに
- [ ] cold　風邪
- [ ] comedian　漫才師、お笑い芸人
- [ ] comic artist　漫画家
- [ ] compare　比較する、比べる
- [ ] comparison　比較、対照
- [ ] computer lab　コンピューター室
- [ ] computer specialist　コンピューター技術者
- [ ] continue　持続する、続ける
- [ ] convenient　便利な
- [ ] conversation　会話
- [ ] cool　カッコいい、イケてる
- [ ] corn dog　アメリカンドッグ
- [ ] costly　値段の高い、高価な
- [ ] cough　咳
- [ ] countryside　田舎
- [ ] coworker　同僚
- [ ] crazy　めちゃくちゃな、おかしい
- [ ] crowded　混雑した、混み合った
- [ ] curly　巻き毛の

D

- [ ] daily life　日常生活
- [ ] dangerous　危ない、危険な
- [ ] dark　濃い
- [ ] definitely　必ず、絶対に
- [ ] delicious　おいしい
- [ ] deliver　配達する、届ける
- [ ] departure point　出発地
- [ ] describe　表す、説明する
- [ ] destination　目的地、行き先
- [ ] dirty　汚い
- [ ] disagree　賛同しない
- [ ] disappoint　がっかりさせる
- [ ] dislikes　嫌いなもの、嫌いなこと
- [ ] downside　悪い点
- [ ] drugstore　薬局、ドラッグストア

E

- [ ] east　東
- [ ] easygoing　のんきな、細かいことを気にしない
- [ ] eat out　外食する
- [ ] echo　繰り返し

Vocabulary List

- [ ] economics　経済学
- [ ] electronics store　電器店
- [ ] energetic　元気な、エネルギッシュな
- [ ] enough　十分な
- [ ] event　出来事、行事
- [ ] example　例
- [ ] exchange student　交換留学生
- [ ] excite　ワクワクさせる、興奮させる
- [ ] exercise　運動する
- [ ] expensive　値段が高い、高価な
- [ ] experience　経験、体験
- [ ] explain　説明する

F

- [ ] fall asleep　眠る
- [ ] family　家族
- [ ] famous　有名な
- [ ] fancy　しゃれた、高級な
- [ ] fast　速い
- [ ] feature　特徴
- [ ] feed　エサを与える
- [ ] feeling　気持ち、思い
- [ ] festival　祭り、催し物
- [ ] fever　熱
- [ ] feverish　熱っぽい
- [ ] fill up　いっぱいにする、満たす
- [ ] fire fighter　消防士
- [ ] fitness center　スポーツジム、体育館
- [ ] fix　直す、修繕する
- [ ] flight　空の旅、飛行、フライト
- [ ] flight attendant　客室乗務員
- [ ] follow-up　あとに続く、追加の
- [ ] food poisoning　食中毒
- [ ] food truck　移動式屋台、キッチンカー
- [ ] foreign　外国の
- [ ] forget　忘れる
- [ ] forgetful　忘れっぽい
- [ ] free time　空き時間、暇なとき
- [ ] French fries　フライドポテト

- [ ] frequency　頻度
- [ ] fresh　新鮮な
- [ ] freshman　1年生
- [ ] friendly　気さくな、フレンドリーな
- [ ] be from …　…出身である
- [ ] funny　おもしろい、楽しい
- [ ] furniture　家具
- [ ] future　未来、将来

G

- [ ] game　ゲーム、試合、競技
- [ ] gargle　うがいをする
- [ ] garlic　ニンニク
- [ ] generous　気前のいい
- [ ] get angry　怒る
- [ ] get fat　太る
- [ ] get married　結婚する
- [ ] get sick　病気になる
- [ ] glasses　眼鏡
- [ ] go back to …　…に帰る、…の元に戻る
- [ ] go for a drink　飲みに行く
- [ ] go on a date　デートする、デートに行く
- [ ] go out　出かける
- [ ] goal　目標、目的
- [ ] goldfish　金魚
- [ ] graduate　卒業する
- [ ] greeting　あいさつ
- [ ] grey　灰色の、グレーの
- [ ] grey hair　白髪
- [ ] grilled　網焼きの、グリルした
- [ ] grow up　育つ

H

- [ ] habit　習慣
- [ ] hang out　連れだって遊ぶ、ぶらぶらする
- [ ] hardly ever …　ほとんど…ない
- [ ] hardworking　勤勉な、よく働く、頑張り屋の

- [ ] hate　ひどく嫌う、大嫌いだ
- [ ] have been to …　…に行ったことがある
- [ ] have never been to …　…に行ったことがない
- [ ] have to …　…しなければならない
- [ ] hay fever　花粉症
- [ ] headache　頭痛
- [ ] health　健康
- [ ] health center　医療センター、医療施設
- [ ] healthcare　医療
- [ ] healthy　健康的な、健康に良い
- [ ] heatstroke　熱中症、熱射病
- [ ] heavy traffic　交通渋滞
- [ ] height　身長
- [ ] historical　歴史のある
- [ ] historical site　史跡
- [ ] hometown　故郷、地元の町
- [ ] hope　希望、願い、見込み
- [ ] hopeless　お手上げな、絶望的な
- [ ] hot springs　温泉
- [ ] hourly pay　時給
- [ ] house party　ホームパーティ
- [ ] househusband　主夫
- [ ] huge　すごく大きい、巨大な
- [ ] hurt　(身体の一部が)痛む

I

- [ ] illness　病気
- [ ] immediately　今すぐに、ただちに
- [ ] impress　感心させる、好印象を与える
- [ ] inconvenient　不便な
- [ ] information systems　情報システム
- [ ] intention　意図、考え
- [ ] interest　興味
- [ ] international student center　留学生センター
- [ ] international tourism　国際観光学
- [ ] introduction　紹介
- [ ] itchy　かゆい

J

- [ ] job　仕事
- [ ] junior　3年生
- [ ] junk food　スナック菓子、ジャンクフード
- [ ] just like ...　ちょうど…のように

K

- [ ] kill　殺す
- [ ] kind　親切な
- [ ] kind of ...　ちょっと…、なんとなく…

L

- [ ] lake　湖
- [ ] later　あとで、後ほど
- [ ] laundry　洗濯
- [ ] law　法学
- [ ] lawyer　弁護士
- [ ] lazy　怠惰な、無精な
- [ ] learning assistance center　学習支援センター
- [ ] least ...　最も…でなく
- [ ] leather goods　皮革製品
- [ ] library　図書館
- [ ] license　免許、資格
- [ ] light　明るい
- [ ] likes　好きなもの、好きなこと
- [ ] live concert　ライブコンサート、ライブ
- [ ] live overseas　海外で暮らす
- [ ] lively　活気のある、活発な、元気な
- [ ] lobster　ロブスター
- [ ] local food　地元の食べ物、郷土料理
- [ ] be located ...　…にある、…に位置する
- [ ] location　位置、場所
- [ ] look forward to ...　…を楽しみにする、…を心待ちにする
- [ ] lose　なくす、失う、減らす
- [ ] lottery　宝くじ
- [ ] loud　うるさい、派手な
- [ ] luxury　ぜいたくな、高級な

M

- [ ] magic trick　手品
- [ ] major　専攻科目
- [ ] major in ...　専攻は…である
- [ ] math　数学
- [ ] mean　意地悪な
- [ ] medicine　薬
- [ ] memorable　記憶に残る
- [ ] middle-aged　中年の
- [ ] midnight　真夜中
- [ ] modern　近代的な、最新の
- [ ] moody　気分屋な
- [ ] move back to ...　…に戻る、(元の場所)に引越す
- [ ] movie　映画
- [ ] movie director　映画監督
- [ ] muscular　筋骨たくましい
- [ ] museum　博物館、美術館
- [ ] mushroom　キノコ
- [ ] mustache　口ひげ

N

- [ ] nap　昼寝、うたた寝、仮眠
- [ ] national reserve　国立保護区
- [ ] nature spot　自然豊かな場所
- [ ] nauseous　吐き気がする
- [ ] need to ...　…する必要がある
- [ ] needs　必要なもの、必要なこと
- [ ] never ...　まったく…ない
- [ ] next to ...　…の隣に
- [ ] night view　夜景
- [ ] noisy　うるさい、騒々しい
- [ ] noon　正午
- [ ] north　北
- [ ] nothing like ...　…とはまるで違っている

O

- [ ] occasionally　たまに
- [ ] office worker　会社員
- [ ] often　よく、たびたび
- [ ] oily　油っぽい
- [ ] on ...th floor　…階にある
- [ ] on time　時間通りに
- [ ] only child　一人っ子
- [ ] opinion　意見
- [ ] optimistic　楽天的な
- [ ] order　注文
- [ ] originally　元は、本来は、生まれは
- [ ] out of style　流行遅れの
- [ ] outgoing　外向的な
- [ ] overcooked　加熱し過ぎた、焼き過ぎた、煮過ぎた
- [ ] overpriced　値段が高すぎる
- [ ] oversleep　寝過ごす
- [ ] overweight　太り過ぎの
- [ ] own　自分の、独自の

P

- [ ] park　公園
- [ ] part-time job　アルバイト
- [ ] pastime　娯楽、気晴らし
- [ ] peaceful　平和な、のどかな、落ち着いた
- [ ] personal information　個人情報
- [ ] personal trainer　個人トレーナー、パーソナルトレーナー
- [ ] personality　性格
- [ ] phone　電話、携帯電話、スマホ
- [ ] plan　計画を立てる、…するつもりだ
- [ ] popular　人気がある、評判がいい
- [ ] Portuguese　ポルトガル語、ポルトガルの
- [ ] positive　積極的な
- [ ] possible　可能な、実行できる
- [ ] prefer ...　…のほうを好む、…がより好きである

- [ ] preference　好み
- [ ] pretty good　なかなかいい、かなり良い
- [ ] price　値段、価格
- [ ] problem　問題
- [ ] professor　教授
- [ ] psychology　心理学

Q

- [ ] question　質問
- [ ] quiet　物静かな

R

- [ ] raw　生の
- [ ] reaction　反応
- [ ] reason　理由
- [ ] reasonable　(値段が) それほど高くない、手頃な
- [ ] recommend　勧める
- [ ] regularly　定期的に
- [ ] reject　拒む、断る、受け入れない
- [ ] reliable　信頼できる
- [ ] remind　思い出させる
- [ ] rent　借りる
- [ ] respond　対応する、応答する
- [ ] rest　休む
- [ ] retirement　引退、退職
- [ ] rice field　水田、田んぼ
- [ ] right away　すぐに
- [ ] river　川
- [ ] roommate　ルームメイト、同居人
- [ ] routine　慣習、日常的に行うこと
- [ ] runny nose　鼻水

S

- [ ] safe　安全な
- [ ] salty　塩辛い、しょっぱい
- [ ] sandy　砂だらけの、ザラザラする
- [ ] satisfy　満足させる
- [ ] save money　貯金する、倹約する
- [ ] scare　怖がらせる
- [ ] scary　怖い
- [ ] scenery　景色、風景、眺望
- [ ] school doctor　校医
- [ ] score　点数、得点
- [ ] senior　4年生
- [ ] serious　真面目な
- [ ] serve　給仕をする、(人のために) 働く、(料理などを) 出す
- [ ] sew　縫う、裁縫をする
- [ ] shark　サメ
- [ ] shopping　買い物
- [ ] short　短い、短期の、背が低い
- [ ] should ...　…すべきである
- [ ] shoulder-length　肩までの長さの、肩に届く
- [ ] shrine　神社
- [ ] shy　恥ずかしがりな
- [ ] sightseeing　観光
- [ ] similarity　類似点
- [ ] skip class　授業をサボる
- [ ] sleepy　眠い
- [ ] slim　細身の、スリムな
- [ ] small talk　おしゃべり、世間話
- [ ] snake　ヘビ
- [ ] snake wine　ヘビ酒
- [ ] sneezing　くしゃみ
- [ ] snowy　雪の多い、雪深い
- [ ] sociable　社交的な
- [ ] social studies　社会科
- [ ] someday　いつの日か
- [ ] sometimes　ときどき
- [ ] somewhere　どこか
- [ ] sophomore　2年生
- [ ] sore throat　のどの痛み
- [ ] sound ...　…のようだ、…のように思える
- [ ] south　南
- [ ] souvenir　みやげ、記念品
- [ ] Spanish　スペイン語、スペインの
- [ ] spicy　辛い
- [ ] spider　クモ、スパイダー
- [ ] sports science　スポーツ科学
- [ ] start one's own business　起業する
- [ ] station　駅
- [ ] stationery　文房具
- [ ] stay　滞在する、留まる
- [ ] stay single　独身でいる
- [ ] stay up late　夜更かしする
- [ ] steal　盗む
- [ ] stingy　けちな、せこい
- [ ] stomach ache　腹痛
- [ ] straight　まっすぐな
- [ ] street food　屋台の料理、露店販売の食べ物
- [ ] strength　強み、得手
- [ ] student affairs office　学生課
- [ ] student life　学生生活
- [ ] study overseas　海外留学する、海外で学ぶ
- [ ] suburb　郊外
- [ ] suggestion　提案、忠告
- [ ] surprise　驚かせる
- [ ] symptom　症状

T

- [ ] tailor　仕立屋、テーラー
- [ ] take a break　休憩する、一息つく
- [ ] tall　背が高い
- [ ] tanned　日焼けした
- [ ] tasty　おいしい、風味がある
- [ ] teenager　(13歳から19歳までの) 10代の若者
- [ ] temple　寺、寺院
- [ ] terrible　ひどい、とんでもない
- [ ] terribly　ひどく、とんでもなく
- [ ] text　メールをする
- [ ] theme park　テーマパーク、遊園地

- [ ] time reference 時間に関する言及、「時」の表現
- [ ] tire 疲れさせる
- [ ] tiring 疲れる
- [ ] together 一緒に
- [ ] tourist 旅行者
- [ ] town 街
- [ ] traditional 伝統的な
- [ ] translator 翻訳家、通訳者
- [ ] transportation 移動手段
- [ ] travel plan 旅行計画
- [ ] trendy 流行の
- [ ] true 真実の、本当の
- [ ] turtle カメ

U

- [ ] unattractive 魅力のない、つまらない
- [ ] unique 個性的な、ユニークな
- [ ] upside 良い点
- [ ] usually いつも、大体

V

- [ ] vacation 休暇
- [ ] view 景色

W

- [ ] wallet 財布
- [ ] wants 欲しいもの、望むこと
- [ ] waste 無駄にする
- [ ] wavy ウェーブのかかった
- [ ] weak point 弱点、欠点
- [ ] weakness 弱み、不得手
- [ ] weekend 週末
- [ ] weight 体重
- [ ] weird 変な、奇妙な
- [ ] west 西
- [ ] whereabouts 位置、所在
- [ ] whistle 口笛を吹く
- [ ] work late 遅くまで働く
- [ ] work out 運動する、体を鍛える
- [ ] worthwhile 価値がある、やりがいのある

Z

- [ ] zoo 動物園

Useful Expressions

- [ ] Are you free …? 「…には時間がありますか」「…はひま?」
- [ ] Certainly. 「かしこまりました」「承知しました」
- [ ] How about …? 「…しませんか」「…はどう?」
- [ ] How many …? 「…はいくつありますか」
- [ ] How often …? 「どのくらいの頻度で…しますか」
- [ ] How was …? 「…はどうでしたか」
- [ ] I can't stand … 「…が我慢できません」「…に耐えられません」
- [ ] I feel … 「…のような気分です」「…みたいな気がする」
- [ ] I see. 「わかりました」「了解」
- [ ] I won the lottery. 「宝くじに当たりました」
- [ ] If I were you, I'd … 「私だったら…します」
- [ ] It's a pleasure to meet you. 「お会いできて嬉しいです」
- [ ] I'll give it a try. 「試してみます」「やってみます」
- [ ] I'm not bad. 「体調は悪くはないです」
- [ ] I'm sorry to hear that. 「それは残念でしたね」「かわいそうに」
- [ ] I'm terribly sorry. 「大変申し訳ありません」
- [ ] Lucky you! 「幸運だったね!」「ラッキー!」
- [ ] No way! 「あり得ない!」「まさか!」
- [ ] Nothing much. 「特に変わったことはありません」「別に」
- [ ] Please call me … 「…と呼んでください」
- [ ] Sounds great. 「とてもいいですね」「すごくいいと思う」
- [ ] Sounds nice. 「いいですね」「いいと思う」
- [ ] Tell me about … 「…について教えてください」
- [ ] That's too bad. 「それはひどいですね」「大変だったね」
- [ ] Uh-huh. 「うん」「そっか」「なるほど」
- [ ] What does he/she look like? 「彼／彼女はどんなかんじ(の容姿)ですか」
- [ ] What is the name of …? 「…の名前は何ですか」
- [ ] What year are you in? 「何年生ですか」
- [ ] What's … like? 「…はどんなかんじですか」
- [ ] What's the best thing about …? 「…の最もいいところは何ですか」
- [ ] What's the worst thing about …? 「…の最も悪いところは何ですか」
- [ ] What's up? 「元気?」「最近どう?」
- [ ] What's wrong? 「どうしたの?」「何かあった?」
- [ ] What's your major? 「専攻は何ですか」
- [ ] Where are you from? 「出身はどちらですか」
- [ ] Why don't we …? 「…するのはどうですか」「…しない?」
- [ ] You're joking! 「冗談でしょ?」「ホントに?」

Photo Credits:

10: (t, l to r) © baona/iStock.com, © eli_asenova/iStock.com, © RyersonClark/iStock.com, (m, l to r) © gorodenkoff /iStock.com, © den-belitsky/iStock.com, © gorodenkoff/iStock.com, (b, l to r) © patpitchaya/iStock.com, © scyther5/iStock.com, © metamorworks/iStock.com; 13: (l) © ajr_images/iStock.com, (r) © ajr_images/iStock.com; 14 (l) © amazingmikael/iStock.com, (r) © violet-blue/iStock.com; 16: (t, l to r) © skynesher/iStock.com, © Wavebreakmedia/iStock.com, © vchal/iStock.com, (m, l to r) © Steve Debenport/iStock.com, © Vasyl Dolmatov/iStock.com, © Jurkos/iStock.com, (b, l to r) © BraunS/iStock.com, © bokan76/iStock.com, © Rawpixel/iStock.com; 26: (t, l to r) © xavierarnau/iStock.com, © shironosov/iStock.com, (mt, l to r) © cdwheatley/iStock.com, © Brzozowska/iStock.com, (mb, l to r) © fotomy/iStock.com, © AndreyPopov/iStock.com, (b, l to r) © Wavebreakmedia/iStock.com, © MASAHIRO_NOGUCHI_NY/iStock.com; 30: (t, l to r) © g-stockstudio/iStock.com, © Deagreez/iStock.com, © andresr/iStock.com, (m, l to r) © Ridofranz/iStock.com, © andresr/iStock.com, © monkeybusinessimages/iStock.com, (b, l to r) © paolo81/iStock.com, © izusek/iStock.com, © Page Light Studios/iStock.com; 36: (t, l to r) © Robert Daly/iStock.com, © djedzura/iStock.com, © Wavebreakmedia/iStock.com, (m, l to r) © william87/iStock.com, © Ababsolutum/iStock.com, © g-stockstudio/iStock.com, (b, l to r) © Sladic/iStock.com, © dwphotos/iStock.com, © vadimguzhva/iStock.com; 42: (t, l to r) © Tijana87/iStock.com, © M_a_y_a/iStock.com, © andresr/iStock.com, (m, l to r) © Steve Debenport/iStock.com, © vadimguzhva/iStock.com, © utah778/iStock.com, (b, l to r) © FatCamera/iStock.com, © Alina555/iStock.com, © TeerawatWinyarat/iStock.com; 52: © leremy/iStock.com; 53: (t, l to r) © JohnnyGreig/iStock.com, © yellowcrestmedia/iStock.com, (b, l to r) © seb_ra/iStock.com, © pixelfit/iStock.com; 57&58: (t, l to r) © seb_ra/iStock.com, © Staras/iStock.com, © Ranta Images/iStock.com, © ElNariz/iStock.com, (m, l to r) © visualspace/iStock.com, © jhorrocks/iStock.com, © Janet Rhodes/iStock.com, © kupicoo/iStock.com, (b, l to r) © kaelhser/iStock.com, © Jacob Ammentorp Lund/iStock.com, © mustafagull/iStock.com, © PeopleImages/iStock.com; 74: (t, l to r) © Minerva Studio/iStock.com, © MStudioImages/iStock.com, © HbrH/iStock.com, (m, l to r) © Weedezign/iStock.com, © lucato/iStock.com, © SeventyFour/iStock.com, (b, l to r) © anouchka/iStock.com, © sisterspro/iStock.com, © Wavebreakmedi/iStock.com; 80: (t, l to r) © SutidaS/iStock.com, © gpointstudio/iStock.com, © artisteer/iStock.com, © malerapaso/iStock.com, (b, l to r) © artisteer/iStock.com, © delihayat/iStock.com, © Wittayayut/iStock.com, © olaser/iStock.com; 86: (t, l to r) © conceptualmotion/iStock.com, © FangXiaNuo/iStock.com, © nortonrsx/iStock.com, (m, l to r) © esolla/iStock.com, © Photobuay/iStock.com, © monkeybusinessimages/iStock.com, (b, l to r) © igor_kell/iStock.com, © SamuelBrownNG/iStock.com, © RapidEye/iStock.com; 97; (l to r) © Takosan/iStock.com, © Starcevic/iStock.com, © BestForLater91/iStock.com; 98; (l to r) © Vladislav Zolotov/iStock.com, © fazon1/iStock.com, © Jui-Chi Chan/iStock.com; 100: (t, l to r) © JohnCarnemolla/iStock.com, © tinnaporn/iStock.com, © narvikk/iStock.com, © alexeys/iStock.com, (b, l to r) © rabbit75_ist/iStock.com, © EarthScapeImageGraphy/iStock.com, © DestinoIkigai/iStock.com, © Franky_Pictures/iStock.com; 103 (l) © rabbit75_ist/iStock.com, (r) © EarthScapeImageGraphy/iStock.com; 104: (l) © JohnCarnemolla/iStock.com, (r) © alexeys/iStock.com; 109: (l to r) © narvikk/iStock.com, © rabbit75_ist/iStock.com, (b, l to r) © tinnaporn/iStock.com, © JohnCarnemolla/iStock.com; 120: © Luisrftc/iStock.com; 122 (t, l to r) © deeepblue/iStock.com, © AntonioGuillem/iStock.com, © hoozone/iStock.com, (m, l to r) © Sasha_Suzi/iStock.com, © PeopleImages/iStock.com, © Zinkevych/iStock.com, (b, l to r) © fizkes/iStock.com, © vadimguzhva/iStock.com, © Image Source/iStock.com; 127: (t, l to r) © Image Source/iStock.com, © Zinkevych/iStock.com, © PeopleImages/iStock.com, (b, l to r) © vadimguzhva/iStock.com, © deeepblue/iStock.com, © AntonioGuillem/iStock.com; 128: (t, l to r) © vadimguzhva/iStock.com, © Sasha_Suzi/iStock.com, © PeopleImages/iStock.com, (b, l to r) © fizkes/iStock.com, © vadimguzhva/iStock.com, © deeepblue/iStock.com; 130: (t, l to r) © Image Source/iStock.com, © monkeybusinessimages/iStock.com, © Digital Vision/iStock.com, © monkeybusinessimages/iStock.com, (m, l to r) © LPETTET/iStock.com, © Image Source/iStock.com, © gorodenkoff/iStock.com, © Highwaystarz-Photography/iStock.com, (b, l to r) © undrey/iStock.com, © Chris Ryan/iStock.com, © torwai/iStock.com, © selimaksan/iStock.com

---

クラス用音声CD有り（別売）

Free Talking
—Basic Strategies for Building Communication

2019年1月20日　初版発行
2025年1月20日　第 6 刷

編著者　Adam Gyenes
著　者　Matthew Guay、Lauren Eldekvist、長谷川由貴
発行者　松村達生
発行所　センゲージ ラーニング株式会社
　　　　〒102-0073　東京都千代田区九段北1-11-11　第2フナトビル5階
　　　　電話 03-3511-4392　FAX 03-3511-4391
　　　　e-mail: eltjapan@cengage.com
　　　　copyright©2019 センゲージ ラーニング株式会社

装　丁　　　足立友幸（parastyle）
編集協力　　飯尾緑子（parastyle）
イラスト　　小川真二郎
印刷・製本　株式会社ムレコミュニケーションズ

ISBN 978-4-86312-349-6

もし落丁、乱丁、その他不良品がありましたら、お取り替えいたします。本書の全部、または一部を無断で複写（コピー）することは、著作権法上での例外を除き、禁じられていますのでご注意ください。